I0568603

Best Day Ever

Stories on Finding Joy
in the Present

a Memoir

By
Tom Rochester

Edited by
Joey Xanders

Gallery Publishing Group

Copyright 2025 by **Tom Rochester**

All rights reserved including the right to reproduce this book or thereof in any form whatsoever. For information, address Gallery Publishing Group Subsidiary Rights Department, 4 Market St 20th Floor San Francisco, CA 94105, USA.

First Gallery Publishing Group Trade Edition November 2025

Special Sales Contact:
For information about special discounts for bulk purchases, please contact Gallery Publishing Group Special Sales at 1-888-929-5571 or robert.williams@gallerypublishinggroup.net

Production Details:
Manufactured in the United States of America

20 19 18 17 16 15 14 13 12

Library of Congress

Cataloging-in-Publication Data is available for the hardcover edition.

E-Book ISBN: 978-1-970989-00-7
Paperback ISBN: 978-1-970989-01-4
Hardcover ISBN: 978-1-970989-02-1

IMAGE CREDITS
Picture on back cover by Joey Xanders.
Cover Design by Andrew Juris.

Margot Rochester was a great teacher, writer, and Mom.

This book pays homage to her legacy.

Praise for
Best Day Ever: Stories of Finding Joy in the Present

"Tom blends practical, hands-on experience with spiritual truths to create inspirational messages that are a breath of fresh air in today's fast-paced, often over-committed world." - **Mike Kayes**

"Tom Rochester writes with his heart and his soul. His stories are powerful, funny, often intimate, and always meaningful. I love his voice and his messages - both are invaluable guides to all of us along our journey towards the best life possible." - **Catherine Florio Pipas, MD, MPH**

"Great lessons from a life well-lived -- insightful, heart-warming and often hilarious!" - **Sarah Cunningham**

"It was a privilege and a pleasure to read these stories. Being a master of self-deprecation, Tom has an endearing way of conveying snapshots of a wonderful life filled with meaningful memories and loving relationships. His desire to share wisdom and experience shines through. I believe we were fortunate to be born into the best generation in history, and these stories remind me of that. The entire book made me smile." - **Donna Ducci**

"Somehow, growing up in the South—where the Flatwater rivers and swamps met the Fall Line, the first unnavigable elevation change on the rivers; where boat traffic stopped and farm goods and merchandise shifted from boat to wagon and vice versa—carries a certain nostalgia." - **Jeff Floyd**

"Reads like a daily devotional. I can see myself reading a story or two a day. They are uplifting stories that teach me about life. I believe they will have a wide appeal to those who want to be motivated, encouraged, and inspired." - **Doug Gray**

"The titles of the stories are terrific. Very creative. I liked the stories I read, and I liked the use of Nuts & Bolts - what a great construct! Thank you for sharing with me, and I truly am impressed and admiring of the efforts and skill that went into this work." - **Barrett Howell**

"From the first chapter to the last chapter, I experienced the evolution of Tom opening up to express his emotional journey, and I teared up a few times. I just loved the easy-breezy reading. I'm 45 years old, and the ideas are pretty much things I know, but I need to hear them from other people, and it helps to hear stories based on Tom's real-life experiences." - **Michelle Freeman**

"I loved the story, "Best Day Ever!" It felt real and heartfelt, made me a bit teary, and was very relatable. I really liked the style of writing, very conversational." - **Dara Greene**

Prologue
Creating A Perfect Story

I am not a huge country music fan. I really liked the music back in the '70s way more than the current stuff. There was a singer-songwriter named David Allen Coe. He was given the lyrics by a songwriter who said it was the perfect country song. David looked at the song lyrics and told his writer friend that the perfect country song would include the words drunk, pickup truck, mom, rain, trains, and prison.

So the writer added the following verse.

> *Well, I was drunk the day my Mom got out of prison*
> *And I went to pick her up in the rain*
> *Before I could get to the station in my pickup truck*
> *She got run over by a damned old train.*

I guess he got it covered—the perfect country and western song.

I thought about how to write a perfect story, what it would include. It depends on where you are from. What subjects you like. I think it would include a lot of humor. Some heartbreak. And at the end, a love which had gone wrong, that somehow had been reconciled. I don't have one of those stories to write on paper.

I was born and raised below the Mason-Dixon line. Way below. South Carolina in the '60s was looked upon by some as a third-world country and considered racist. Yearning for different civil war results. Uneducated. Some of which is true. I grew up in a small town in the middle of South Carolina. I share many of my observations from growing up in the following pages of my book. I don't know much about folks from other places. Assume they have stories, too. Here in the South, we have stories. Some of them are true. It's a well-known fact here in the South that if you don't have a story for a situation, you just make one up. But I want to assure you that all mine are semi-factual. Sometimes exaggerated. But that's to make it a little more enjoyable to read.

Frequently, I make myself out to be the hero. Why not put on paper something that makes you look more impressive than you are in real life? I learned a lot about storytelling from my Dad. I loved sitting in the den hearing him share episodes of his military experiences. He could tell them so well that you felt like you were present when they happened. It made me proud. He shared a lot of other stories, too. I should have written them down.

I was my Mom's favorite. She never showed favoritism, but I knew it. She lived a life like no other. She was brilliant but didn't need to show off. I'd like people to think about me being brilliant, but I know that's not true. She could tell stories, too. She could write them even better. She could use words I'd never heard, but I will never forget. She had a doctorate in creative writing. Mom could have authored the book on storytelling. She also wrote gardening articles for hometown newspapers across the country.

My brother was two years younger. I could not have imagined better adolescent years, sharing a room with him. Of course, we didn't have Instagram to tell us that life could be any different. What we had were the surroundings of scrub oaks, pine trees, and poison oak. We have lots of voices of other young children in the neighborhood. TV was limited. At my house, we had a single channel on a black-and-white TV. You don't have to spend a lot of time arguing about what to watch when there is only one channel. There was a library in school that provided me with a lot of stimulation. I liked biographies and gangster books the most. My fascination with gangster books always had my Mom concerned. Regardless, she encouraged me to read. And I did, starting with Rolling Stone magazine in 1973. Up until 1980, I read every issue from cover to cover. Rolling Stone was where I first encountered many ideas and perspectives from places that were beyond my small town in South Carolina.

Reading and hearing require a human being to tap into a part of their brain that watching just can't do. It's hard to get your head around something that you cannot see. However, I could listen to a football game and feel as if I were on the 50-yard line. But growing up in a town that could be called Simpleville provided more experiences than the State Fair. Pictures would do a better job of sharing my upbringing. A movie wouldn't be necessary. It would be pretty ordinary. Humanity seems to grow tired of the ordinary. They prefer the dysfunctional and unpredictable. My parents had enough in each other's presence. Not needing anything more than they could afford. Dad was frugal. Imagine many children saying that about their Dad.

As you read my words, I hope you get a picture of how I grew up. Why I see things the way I do. Consider sending me a story so I can hear about your existence here on this planet. Relationships improve when storytelling is included in our conversations. Can't wait to listen to yours.

A Note to My Readers

A little more about me. I recently retired from running a successful construction materials business. I have been blessed with a great family, great friends, and a strong faith that leads me to believe there is something better ahead. I have too many passions. I love golf, hunting, shooting, going to the gym, and most importantly, having a good conversation. I really like talking to strangers. I really like sharing funny stories. I've been broke, and I've been flush, and I've found that you can find enjoyment in either financial state. My mindset is the same regardless of my bank account. I've had bright days and dark days. I've learned more from setbacks than from victories. In my 65 years on earth, I've witnessed many things and enjoyed the voyage, potholes, and all.

As I mentioned, I was born and raised in South Carolina, the son of two loving parents. They lived within their modest means, and where I come from, a mansion was any house two stories high. Mom worked in marketing and transitioned into school teaching once I was of middle school age. My father was a forester and moved us to where the timber was plentiful, to the South, in the late 50s. In that era, outsiders were quickly identified by their northern accents and excluded from the camaraderie by their new neighbors. However, my parents seemed to wander through the maze of Southern culture by adapting to local ways without compromising their character or values. Mom and Dad never embraced the underlying racism of the South, which is one of many reasons I am proud to be their son.

Six years ago, I made a list of what I wanted to do with my time. I listed playing an instrument, volunteering, learning to fly, focusing on golf, and writing my stories. COVID made it easy.

There are fewer distractions when we are told not to leave our yard. It reminded me of being grounded during my teenage days. So, I wrote.

I used a canary yellow legal pad and wrote in cursive. Frequently, I wrote on the porch overlooking my backyard. It inspired me to write with more intensity—something about the great outdoors with a pen in hand. Occasionally, a bigger word would appear in my mind, something that I had always wanted to write on paper. My handwriting is awful. I would read my chicken scratch into a microphone that would transcribe the words into a digital version of the story. Many times, I had to stop and work to interpret my handwriting. I should have spent more time working on penmanship as a child. After a few years, I had a pile of short pieces that became this book.

Often, I'd visit a local Starbucks and write there. One day, the manager asked me what I was writing about. I told her it was a collection of short stories meant to entertain, amuse, and provoke reflection—a fancy way of saying we should sit still and ponder what our lives are about. The intention of my writing is to bring awareness that the best day ever is today—the one we have right now. The manager said she'd be interested in a book like that.

So that's one reader. My children will be required to read this book in order to get their inheritance. That makes three more. My wife has indicated that she doesn't fall into the required reader category. She'll probably skim the book to fact-check my exaggerations.

I hope this book inspires you to have a great day. That may seem like a tall order, but I believe it's possible. A couple of years ago, my grandkids, a girl who was then four and a boy who was 6, came to visit from far away. My wife, Cindy, and I planned all sorts of activities to make their stay memorably fun. A few days in, we sat around the breakfast table, and one of the kids started chanting, "Best day ever!" Soon, everyone joined in, and we were all yelling in unison, "Best day ever," laughing ourselves silly. It was magic. And just like that, it became our mantra—our new way to start each day.

That experience moved me and got me thinking. What if we approached every day with the mindset that it could be a great day! I decided to make a list of what it would take. Topping the list was a morning cup of coffee in silence, closely followed by spending quality time with my wife. Going to the gym was on that list. Doing a good deed or two. Meeting certain goals at work. I encourage you to consider your own list of what would make today a great day for you, and see if you can make those things happen.

In the following pages, I will offer reminders, some of which you might have heard before but find helpful to hear again. I'd like my experiences, takeaways, and encouragement to serve as food for thought. At the end of each story, you'll find a section I call "Nuts and Bolts," where I share some of the things I've learned (a lot of them the hard way; some of them the funny way) about what it takes to build a good life. Enjoy.

Table of Contents

CHAPTER 1

When I Was Young

Childhood Stories

Story 1
The Lure of Fishing

My Dad was a fisherman at heart. He often dragged his boat with us wherever we went on vacation. Typically, our trips were poorly planned, while our equipment list was meticulous. My Dad would have 60 items written on a canary yellow pad of paper, as well as two motors in the boat, because he had contingency plans for every potential mishap. However, we would go to places without making any reservations. Dad didn't want to waste money on a long-distance call to reserve a room. As a result, we would trek from hotel to hotel, hoping to get a room. We went in a direction and then decided that where we ended up was where Dad had intended to go all along.

My parents had vastly different ideas about what constituted a vacation. Dad's idea of a vacation was to sit at the boat store repairing motors and talking with friends all afternoon. He had no desire to leave his driveway to see the world. My mother, on the other hand, was more of a dreamer. She relished the gatherings where neighbors would showcase the latest carousel of slides documenting their recent adventures and trips. They shared stories of the South Carolina coast and the North Carolina mountains, home to the Tweetsie Railroad—often described as the Disney World of the Carolinas' highlands. We were always one slide carousel behind where others had been. Mom hoped to catch up one day.

Because Dad failed to plan, he'd often have to give a pep talk to rally my Mom, my younger brother, Dan, and me back onto the proverbial team bus. Sometimes, we thought it might have been better just to stay home. And Dad decided to do that one day. It was our Christmas vacation, the car was packed, and his 60 items on the canary yellow pad were checked off. We were sitting in the car, ready to reverse out of the driveway. Suddenly, Dad turned to us and said, "I have a bad omen. We shouldn't go." Mom was not happy. She complained and moaned while Dad stayed firm. We weren't going. We piled out of the car and back into the house. The next day, Dad reconsidered and said we should go. He couldn't get any of us in the car. We stayed home, and we kids were happy, for our preference was to play with friends.

Except that is, when we ended up on Ocracoke Island off North Carolina, Dad's favorite vacation spot, and a great destination.

On our first Ocracoke vacation when I was 10 years old, Dad launched his 18-foot Jon boat into the Atlantic, and we went to an area where fishermen congregated. It was a beautiful sight. The Ocracoke boats were built of wood and painted white. However, our boat wasn't white, and there were many times when people would ask us to move our boat out of the frame so the photographer could get the picturesque shot of the white boats on the water. Dad was often not willing to comply.

We observed these boats catching lots of fish and were eager to do the same. It looked easy. Of course, we used our lures brought from home, but it turned out that the scaly creatures had no interest in them. We were discouraged, and it wasn't so fun because now we were the have-nots. Dad set out to solve the problem of figuring out how to fill our boat with fish. He had to do some research, but you need to understand, we were clearly not from the area. This put us at quite a disadvantage, and if not handled properly, there would be no secret divulged on how to catch these fish. Dad knew we were wildly unprepared for this endeavor. It was like we were wearing t-shirts and shorts to a black tie affair. We did not belong.

However, my Dad could get people to participate in a discussion they had no intention of participating in. His gift was the art of conversation. He knew how to create a dialogue and have the other person leave feeling good. He got people to trust him. I've never experienced this phenomenon again in my life. Only my Dad knew how to ask questions and get others to share information without making them feel he was imposing. He had the gift of listening, of asking the right questions. Finally, he conveyed to the locals that we were good folks who were trying really hard.

He used our underdog status to become endeared to the local people, who then wanted to help us. You think I'm a talker? I'm nothing compared to my Dad. With this gift of gab he was able to extract from them the missing magic weapon that would allow us the glory of a fish dangling from our line: a three and a quarter inch Hopkins lure that could be acquired at Tradewinds Tackle Shop.

Later that day, we walked into Tradewinds Tackle, eager to find the key to our days of fun. I should mention that I have never been overly passionate about fishing, but I do enjoy reeling them in. Guess most people like the catching part of fishing. We found the tackle aisle, and there in front of us lay the silver bullet: the three-and-a-quarter-inch Hopkins lure sparkling before our eyes. It featured a metallic, spoon-like design, with a slightly curved body that helped it mimic the movement of injured baitfish in the water. There were bright, reflective colors, with patterns like silver, gold, or chartreuse to attract fish. Its weighted body ensured long casts so we could target the coveted speckled trout. The sharp treble hook looked like a fish magnet. We couldn't wait.

Something else that caught our attention was the fluorescent orange price tag that read $3.25. Mind you, this was 1972, and $3.25 was a lot of money for the Rochester family. My Dad was frugal—he even studied the grocery store receipts that Mom brought home. He faced a dilemma. Was he going to step up and spend the money needed to make this a memorable vacation? You

4

know how sometimes you can read someone's mind? I sensed he was going to give in to the pressure. Hey, you only live once! He decided to buy four of them—one for each fisherman: Dad, Dan, and me, plus one as a reserve in the unlikely event that one of us lost this powerful weapon.

The next morning, as we got into our boat among all the local vessels, we stood out like a sore thumb. Our boat was neither wooden nor white. It was an aluminum, green-painted boat. It identified us as flatlanders, a euphemism for being a tourist. Nobody wants to appear as a tourist. We meandered out to the sweet spot where all the other boats were testing their Hopkins lures. The boats essentially lined up in the water to be moved out to the fishing zone by the tide in order. We were a bit nervous because our only hope of catching any fish was if they made room for us in this order. Dad's goodwill extended with the locals, and even though they generally resented tourists, they were quietly rooting for us. There were others who would not be included in the reindeer games, and never have been accepted at face value– but somehow, they made room for us. We were given a shot. They'd even call over, "How y'all doing over there?" From my Dad, I learned that Southern style is about letting the conversation come to you. Don't try to direct it in a self-serving direction; just let it unfold.

Now, I hoped the Hopkins lure was irresistible. I tried to imagine what it would be like to be a fish with a shiny, bug-like thing jiggling out in front of me. But before we could start, Dad had to lecture my brother and me on economics. He held up one of the valuable hooked pieces of metal and stated, "Boys, these lures cost $3.25 each." He didn't need to say, "Don't lose it;" we understood the implication. My brother and I were so traumatized that we tied about eight knots each to secure our line to the treasured device. Then, we both tentatively dropped it off the side of the boat, maybe a couple of feet below the surface. That way, we wouldn't be putting the lure in harm's way. Of course, we also wouldn't be catching any fish. But we were walking on eggshells, fearing we would be the one to lose a lure.

Dad reared back and let his lure fly. I bet it went 100 yards—no kidding, 100 yards. I saw a small splash so far away that I couldn't believe it had traveled so far. I was really amazed and proud. He started to reel in his prized fish-catching machine. Dan and I were amused because we both noticed his line bouncing off the top of the water, which was mysterious. After all, the lure should have been pulling the line deep. When my Dad got the line close to the boat, he saw that his lure might have gone 100 yards, but his line had not. Line and lure had parted ways. The reason the lure went so far is that it didn't have anything tied to it. The lure was lost.

My brother and I stared at the water. We knew that if we looked at our Dad, we would laugh uncontrollably, so we kept our gazes averted. Dad realized that his initial casting had resulted in the very thing we feared most: the loss of the $3.25 Hopkins lure. He lifted the limp line and blurted out, "Boys, let that be a lesson to you."

Actually, I believe it was divine intervention. God untied that knot so that we could have one of the most memorable fishing trips ever. He wanted us to learn to relax and remember we are supposed to be having fun. The rest of the day went perfectly. Fish were caught, dinner was had, and the fourth Hopkins lure was just as good as the second and third ones. Later, over a trout dinner, Dad said he lost the lure on purpose to make us feel better. We didn't begrudge him his little white lie because, deep down, it was just his way of trying to save face in front of his boys and to show that he cared.

Let that be a lesson to you. I heard my father say it several times in my childhood. It typically followed an attempt to explain some effort of his that did not go as planned.

Nuts and Bolts: There's a lesson to be learned here—the very fact that there are lessons to be learned. You don't have to experience all of life's mishaps yourself; you can learn from others. Whether it's relationships, poor decisions, or even unexplained events like my Dad's cast, life doesn't always go as planned—it just doesn't. We laughed, we relaxed, and we went about enjoying our day. We created wonderful memories. Lastly, I learned that in the South, you don't chase the conversation. You wait for it to find you. No angles, no agendas—just let it take shape on its own.

Story 2
Kind of Like This

I recall another vacation out on the coast to Ocracoke, North Carolina, when I was about eleven or twelve. We were taking this trek as part of our annual summer two-week vacation. There was a lot of space between the crossroads, and we saw pine trees going on forever. We know it was my Dad's favorite place away from home; truth be told, it was Mom's, too. I secretly would have preferred to stay home with my friends. That beach was desolate; there was just no one there. No Ferris wheel. No arcades. Just 13 miles of National Seashore beach without any signs of humanity. Later in life, I grew to enjoy the solitude. But back when I was a kid, I just missed my friends.

As usual, my Dad had his canary yellow pad filled with checklists of necessary items. My Mom, my brother, and I were not checklist people. My Mom's approach to life was to be kind, and she had faith that others would be kind in turn. If anything went amiss, God had our backs. Interestingly, her approach seemed to work better than his. Things went wrong even though Dad went to great extremes to prevent them, but somehow, we always landed on our feet.

We were in eastern North Carolina, between towns, hauling Dad's 18-foot Jon boat. All of a sudden, the back wheel of the boat trailer locked up, and I could see smoke coming off it. We came to a screeching halt. I remember feeling a bit traumatized, wondering how we were going to get this fixed. My Dad had his yellow pad list, and I guess greasing the bearings wasn't on it. It's funny how, out in the country, people seem to have more time. We all have 24 hours in a day, but I think country folks just know how to use those hours more effectively. Before I knew it, we had our own eastern North Carolina rescue team. Somehow, we managed to get off the road. I remember a BBQ joint about 100 yards ahead. We wandered over there, and my Dad got help from the barbecue restaurant owner. I've shared with you that my Dad was one of the greatest talkers of all time.

It was either a Saturday or Sunday, late in the day, long after we should have been able to find help. Oh, it couldn't have been Sunday because, during that era in the Carolinas, nonessential businesses were not allowed to be open. They called them Blue Laws. They originated way back, like in colonial America, and aimed to preserve the day for rest. Sundays were sacred. You wouldn't even cut your yard on Sunday. This must sound nostalgic, but being forced by government regulations to be still helped us focus on what's more important than commerce, like relationships.

Somehow, Dad got on the phone and called a neighbor of the owner of the vinegar and pepper sauce BBQ restaurant. Not mustard-based or tomato-based, just vinegar and peppers, North Carolina BBQ. Then, out of nowhere, a man in coveralls shows up. He jumps out of a pickup truck and asks, "How you doing?" Clearly, we weren't doing so well at the moment. He had an acetylene torch and started the involved process of heating the axle to free the wheel. Other than that, I can't remember much of the process of fixing the wheel. I was only 12 back then, and now I'm over 60. I can't believe I remember what I do. At any rate, it's always a surprise when someone not part of the scene decides to step up and help. You expect it of friends and family. I don't know how other people feel, but I have received more kindness from strangers than I can count.

As our newfound friend worked on the tire, we were drawing a crowd. It wasn't typical to see a stranger around there, and this was more entertaining than television. In the audience were three really pretty girls. I mean, really pretty. They were genuinely nice

9

to me. At 12 years old, you're kind of interested in girls. You definitely didn't want your parents to know about it. I wanted to act really cool. But I didn't know how. I responded by being really shy and making no eye contact. They were older than I was - already looking grown up, if you know what I mean. While I don't remember how the tire got fixed, I do remember those three girls.

Back to the trailer crisis. Well, not quite yet. The restaurant owner came out with barbecue sandwiches for the whole family and wouldn't hear of getting paid. Now, that was really kind. I'm starting to hear myself talking and writing with a Southern accent. Stretch out the pronunciation of the words as you read, y'all.

It was getting dark. I wondered if my Dad had budgeted any money to stay in a trailer court hotel within a short ride. Turns out we didn't need to. The man who appeared out of nowhere had fixed the tire problem. I remember Dad reaching into his tight wallet and pulling out what felt like a fortune—a $10 bill. He reached out appreciatively to pay the man, but the man refused it. He said he was glad to help, and he truly meant it. There was no need to push the subject any further.

That's a truly random act of kindness. There were lots of participants. I liked the pretty girls most. I also liked the barbecue and the coverall-wearing angel who showed up to save our vacation.

Nuts & Bolts: It's been 50 years, and I still remember the angels who saved our day. It takes time and sometimes may make you late for dinner, but try to brighten someone's day. Being an angel can be risky, so be cautious. However, for the most part, angelic behavior pays off. It feels good to be kind. We can't afford to let this four-letter word slip from our vocabulary. Heck, let's make it go viral.

Story 3
Animal Crackers on Aisle 1

I was standing at the entrance of a Publix store recently, realizing that those plastic rectangles in the child seats are still part of the shopping experience, never to be improved. Some things are just that way. It reminded me of grocery shopping memories with my Mom. I can still picture the red A&P sign, which represented a cutting-edge shopping experience. A&P was a leading grocery store chain that became obsolete in the early '70s. The weekly trip turned into an event I always looked forward to.

Mom would pick me up and slide my legs through the openings in the shopping cart. This allowed me to sit down and view the store from a different angle. Mostly, though, I just saw my Mom. I liked seeing her. I have many memories from that time. Once I was settled in the shopping cart, my main reason for looking forward to the trip was right there in aisle one: animal crackers. My Mom was a people pleaser, so I could easily persuade her to grab a box of those tasty, animal-shaped cookies quickly. The elephants were my favorites, but they all tasted alike. I wasn't the only toddler who convinced their Mom that this was a necessary purchase. It seemed like every kid would point to the stack of this critical food group before they could talk.

Mom would go from aisle to aisle, buying things, chatting with a couple of folks, and finally making our way to the cash register to deal with the financial consequences of reaching up on the shelves and filling our cart.

And as I got older, I ended up with a younger brother who usurped my throne inside the shopping cart. Sometimes, when I whined loudly enough, my Mom would let me sit in the grocery section of the cart. I'm not sure if she did this out of sympathy or just to get me to stop whining. My Mom said I was a good whiner, which I suppose is a compliment. I never considered adding it to my resume, but looking back, I see that it might have turned out to be a valuable business skill. I'll have to think about that.

I didn't understand why I needed a younger brother. We were perfectly happy, just the three of us. But I didn't get a vote. However, there was a benefit to being downgraded to a walker instead of a rider. I could get my own animal crackers, which was pretty nice for gaining independence. Plus, I would eat half of my brother's cookies, too. I guess this was my first venture into salesmanship — convincing Dan that he didn't need the whole box of cookies after all. I didn't even have to use coercion. This might have contributed to me wearing Husky pants at an early age, with 'Husky' being a polite '60s way of saying 'fat.' But getting an extra half box of differently shaped animal dough was worth it.

As I grew out of my animal cracker habit, I moved on to other sugary distractions. The candy display at the checkout counter was pure evil. Why do they put this unnecessary temptation right there where it can't be avoided? It ruins a perfectly good shopping experience for moms. Did I mention I was quite the whiner? Or am I just a salesperson? I'm sure I was annoying. I can still be a little noisy sometimes. I'd plead that if I didn't get a bag of M&M's, I would die of malnutrition. I'm sure my Mom understood the essentials of a good diet, but most of the time, she relented. I loved my Mom. Come to think of it, I've found a lot of M&M wrappers in my wife's car, too. I guess children's persuasion skills remain alive and well.

My Mom, or Margot, as the adults called her, became a school teacher once I reached the age where I was a student. She was a rock star in the classroom, recognizing the potential in every student, even when the students themselves didn't see it. Later, she began writing gardening articles for a newspaper and then for several other newspapers, back when they mattered. Her style was folksy yet grammatically correct. She ended up publishing a couple of gardening books, one of which was featured on the cover of the Walmart book page, though it was soon overshadowed by Bill Clinton's book, "My Life." I guess politics is seen as more important than gardening. She appeared on NPR on Saturdays in different cities. I remember calling her, and she told me she was in Boston that day, but it was only her voice on the radio. She was in her room at home, sitting at her kitchen table, answering questions about her life and gardening. I didn't know much about her fan base until her death, when so many of her followers came to say goodbye.

This story runs through my mind while I'm still standing at the entry of a Publix store. I realize those rectangles in the seat are still part of the shopping experience, never to be improved. Some things are just that way–they don't change. I considered climbing in the cart and reliving my animal cracker experience. After giving it some thought, I opted just to write about it. They would have called security to assist in removing an old man stuck in a grocery cart. Maybe banned me from the store. That would be annoying.

Nuts & Bolts: Mom's love was unconditional. She put up with my whining and even turned it into a compliment. She made grocery shopping into a pleasant experience that I remember fondly to this day. It's difficult these days to avoid dwelling on life's challenges, and I acknowledge that some issues are unavoidable. However, we can also create time to appreciate our blessings, past and present. Writing them down is a great start. And just maybe you'll rediscover your own animal cracker/Mom story that is part of your legacy.

Story 4
You Do Not Talk About Fight Club

My Dad loved boxing when I was a child. So much so that I remember Dad coming home from work one day with little, brown, padded vinyl material, which I learned later were boxing gloves. Soon enough, we were in the backyard, each of us wearing a pair, and he began teaching me the basics. Avoid getting hit being the most important. I was not good at that. He showed me how to keep my shoulders square and my fists compact —the essentials of being a good boxer.

Don't get me wrong–I had a great Dad and a wonderful childhood. I respect my father's efforts to toughen us up in preparation for a challenging world. My Dad enjoyed watching me mix it up with my brother and, often, with other kids in the neighborhood. Dad supervised these matches and made sure our blows were civil. Above the belt, so to speak.

I can recall one fight we hosted in my backyard. There were several kids there. We were all apprehensive about boxing. The fear of getting hit and the fear of losing made us reluctant. Now that I think about it, getting hurt intentionally is probably why we didn't raise our hands first. This match, like most of our matches, had very little contact. My strategy was to wear out my opponent by having him exhaust himself swinging at me and missing. One thing I didn't mind, however, was getting hit once, maybe twice. This approach to boxing will definitely shorten your career. The intent, after all, is to avoid getting hit at all. Once my opponent grew tired of swinging and missing or swinging and getting a punch or two in, I was much more likely to succeed in getting my couple of punches in.

I know this whole scenario sounds barbaric, but it worked for me. I'd highly recommend a different strategy if you're ever boxing. I was declared the winner when Johnny ran out of the ring. It was not a ring, really. We identified a square that wasn't even marked. Maybe it was marked by a group of trees.

Yes, I did win some of those altercations. Lost some, too. Don't get me wrong–these weren't fights like Brad Pitt in Fight Club. Can you imagine parents encouraging this kind of activity now? Back in the seventies, there were no consent forms to fill out. Needless to say, even then, some parents didn't necessarily approve of this activity.

My Dad had to tone it down after a few kids went home and shared what they did at Tom's house, which raised some eyebrows. We started getting phone calls from concerned parents about the activities that upset their children after a bout in our backyard. It's not as if anyone was performing exorcisms; they were simply engaging in uncharacteristic activities. One father in the neighborhood was upset because he said his son was forced to put on the gloves. He was no longer included in our "Fight Club."

No one received permanent physical or emotional damage from our gatherings. There were no benefits at all, and no one made us participate. The lesson I learned from my early boxing experiences is that life requires you to hang in there and be persistent, even when there's some pain involved. If there were no discomfort, then there'd be no need to think about persistence in the first place. It's the struggle, the discomfort, the persistence – that's where growth happens.

Nuts & Bolts: Persistence is essential in developing innovative ideas, athletic prowess, or successful collaboration with others. Reflecting on this writing, I probably picked a bad example by choosing children boxing. Well, sometimes in life, that happens, too. The point is that everything valuable demands effort. Thus, when contemplating giving up on education, career, marriage, parenting, diet, or anything important to you, look to the horizon. It is closer than you think. Some of your endeavors may fall by the wayside, and that's okay. But do seek out passions in life that require you to toil. You'll come out better for it.

Story 5
Measure Twice, Mentor Once

When I was growing up, a neighbor across the street was a big help to me. This neighbor, Don, was very willing to help me solve the mysteries of math. This process became a biweekly experience. I'm surprised I didn't wear a path between our houses. However, I was always welcomed whenever I needed help. My early memories of my neighbor include that he was very smart for an adult, that he looked me in the eye, and that he used big words. I often saw him outside cutting the lawn or trimming the hedges. He had a very nice yard.

Our neighborhood was idyllic for a kid. It felt like a village where ranch houses had borders but no fences. Wherever you landed, you'd get a peanut butter sandwich and Kool-Aid in a jelly jar. Calling dibs meant you snagged the Fred Flintstone jar, the most sought-after prize. The inevitable arguments were settled by a Mom who made the final decision.

Don's home was one of the places where we landed for peanut butter sandwiches, but he never participated in the lunch ceremony. Instead, Don's role was to help the Rochester family, whose family tree lacked a mathematician. For our part, we possessed other notable family traits: we were good storytellers and relatively athletic individuals. In high school, once my grades started coming in, my parents had no doubt I was their child. As long as we had enough fingers and toes, we could hold our own with the best of them. But algebra isn't a fingers-and-toes subject. My parents sent me to Don across the street.

As I grew older, I realized Don had a very successful career as an engineer. He had more patents than anyone short of Tom Edison.

It didn't matter that he was accomplished; I was always a priority, and he was never distracted when we were together. Working with Don was an opportunity to have someone address my math shortcomings. Don's body language showed so much patience that I didn't feel rushed. He asked provocative questions that led me to the correct answers, rather than just showing me the answer. I learned to process information instead of memorizing it.

We worked through 9th-grade math—successfully, too. I started getting A's. And, it changed my life direction. With Don's help, I met the math requirements for engineering, which ultimately led to my successful career as a construction company owner. Don's willingness to give and share his time with me twice a week for months on end is one brick in the foundation of my successful life.

I got to memorialize Don recently. I was telling this story at his funeral, and the family was shocked. It really heartened them to learn what their Dad did. I was most surprised to understand that they didn't even remember seeing me learning this stuff. How could they not know?

They had recollections of us playing basketball in the front yard or their Dad helping me repair my late model automobile, which I was incapable of doing on my own. The experience of me sitting on their green vinyl couch with a math book in my lap and their Dad on my side escaped their memory. It's amazing how often we overlook the impact of ordinary moments.

His funeral was a celebration. His purpose here was fulfilled. And this story is a tribute to his generosity.

Nuts and Bolts: This experience reminded me that even in the most ordinary moments, we have the chance to make a meaningful impact on someone's life. I was fortunate to have a neighbor who did just that—Don's influence left a lasting mark on my future. We all have gifts, and I'm grateful Don didn't keep his to himself. He taught me that part of our purpose in life is to look beyond our own needs and serve others. As long as we're here—alive and breathing—we're called to reach back and bring others along on the journey.

Our paths may differ, but the walk through life becomes richer when we support one another, whether we're offering help or receiving it. So, look for those quiet chances to use your gifts for good. The world—and you—will be better for it.

Story 6
Riding In The Back

It's always been my habit to talk to virtually everyone on a plane. The people to my left and right are my best friends for two hours. Business gurus would tell you successful people sit in the front of the plane—a networking opportunity. However, I find the back of the vehicle to be the best place to engage with fellow travelers. Philosophically, it's a symbolic gesture to allow others to go in front of you. It reflects a humility that many of us talk about but don't act upon nearly as frequently as we should. By declaring myself to be ordinary, I have the most in common with other travelers on this journey called life.

On a more practical level, the sad truth is that nobody communicates on planes anymore, particularly in first class. Ear buds seem to be everyone's favorite privacy screen. Or maybe they serve as a sign saying, Don't bother me. Probably directed right at me. As for myself, I strike up conversations. Not like John Candy in the 1987 film "Planes, Trains and Automobiles," but I do like finding out where my new neighbor is going. What takes them there? And maybe a few other questions. Nothing too serious, though. I always enjoy meeting a new person, even when the conversation takes a surprising turn.

One day, a lovely young woman sat next to me in row 29. She was a striking woman, and I had high expectations of our conversation (I'm fine admitting my bias!). I could hear the plane buzzing with conversation as she and I chatted. I was enjoying the flow when we somehow got talking about religious activities. I mentioned I was a Methodist attendee. She asked me, "When were you saved?" At the top of her lungs! The entire plane fell so quiet that you could hear a pin drop. I was 25 years old and didn't know how to respond. Most Baptists can state the day and time when they were saved. I know it might be hard to believe, but at this point, people on the plane stopped to listen to my answer. The buzz died, and the plane was absolutely quiet, awaiting my reply.

I'm sure I stuttered as I said something along the lines of how Methodists don't proclaim a specific day when we accept Jesus Christ as our Savior, unless one has a lightning bolt experience, which I haven't. We were having a pleasant conversation, and this stranger had decided to delve into my faith life. I felt as if I needed to make a testimony. It's like asking me about my W2 or my sex life—way too intimate. She seemed ready to baptize me right there on the damn airplane. She meant well. It just didn't feel like the right time. I hope my fellow travelers were satisfied as I squirmed to create a soft landing.

On a different trip, my expectations were turned upside down. You know how you walk to the vicinity of your gate, you scan the other passengers, and immediately you identify the ones you would appreciate not sitting next to? In this case, I was flying back from Dallas and noticed a heavy-set Hispanic gentleman wearing flower shorts and a wife-beater. Well, he was my seatmate. I immediately considered my discomfort sitting with this new not-bestfriend as I tried to squeeze into my seat. Regardless of my bias, I engaged my seatmate and discovered he had an interesting career traveling to different sound studios around the country working with musicians. He had experiences that I would have loved to have had. He listed musicians that I didn't recognize because he was young and hip, but I could tell his life allowed him to be up close and connected to the adventure of creating music. I had completely misjudged this expectation and reminded myself not to judge a book by its cover. I considered myself lucky that I had stuck to my principle of finding a seat in the back, which enabled this lovely encounter.

Regardless of the challenges, I still firmly believe that economy class is the best option for gregarious folks like me and for enriching your life experiences. By the way, I have never seen any cattle or loose chickens back there. Over the years, I have even gotten a couple of good book recommendations and new bands to listen to. I also met little Johnny(or JB as his Dad called him), a screaming two-year-old who reminded me of my child-rearing days. It can be nostalgic to sit in the back.

My first acquaintance with sitting in the back began in elementary and middle school. The new students were always relegated to the back of the school bus. That's where we would be properly hazed on our 20-minute ride to be educated. We came up with all kinds of stuff to torment and tease each other, and shorten the trip – all in good fun. Some activities would probably be called assaults nowadays, i.e., the wedgie was always a favorite for a newcomer on the bus. And a good old haystack never hurt anyone. That's when all the kids would jump on you until you were at the bottom of this pile, unable to breathe. They would finally unstack themselves, and you felt properly humiliated amongst your young peers.

When I was in the first grade, I remember being the victim of someone sticking gum in my hair. He said it was an accident. And I was too little to challenge him. After that, I befriended a sixth-grade girl who could be meaner than a snake and was bigger than most of the guys. Thanks to this guardian angel, I never had any gum in my hair again. My life changed. I no longer feared getting on that bus where I would suffer from these abuses. I had found an ally.

Nuts & Bolts: The back of the bus brings back some childhood rites of passage that I can look back on fondly. As for plane travel, if you typically find yourself bemoaning your seat in the back of the plane, maybe turn lemons into lemonade. Try the toned-down John Candy approach and engage your seatmate. It might change your life. And, if you're lucky enough to be seated in first class, maybe consider swapping with one of those economy sitters. Seek out someone who could benefit from your generosity - a senior citizen, someone serving in the military, an immigrant. Small gestures can have a profound impact on lives. Lastly, consider having your life story ready in your back pocket.

CHAPTER 2

Testing the Boundaries

Stories from the College Years

Story 1
Making a Splash

I have a thing about water. Not a phobia—just the opposite. But I don't like taking long showers. This lead-in is an excuse to discuss my first day at Clemson University in South Carolina. After a night of overindulging, I woke up and turned on the faucet, but no water came out. The water had been shut off. I shrugged and walked away. Apparently, I forgot to shut off the faucet once I discovered there was no water. When the water came back on, it quickly overfilled the sink, then overflowed into my room, and eventually soaked every other student's room. I was out enjoying the day on campus, watching coeds and hoping they would be eager to meet a brand-new addition to the campus. When I returned to the dorm, I noticed the hall carpet squishing underneath my tennis shoes. I didn't know any of my new neighbors, but I was quickly introduced in a way I wished hadn't happened. I wanted to blend in slowly—nothing like a big splash into the neighborhood. I remember a life jacket being taped to my door the next morning. That was followed by notes advertising swimming lessons. Of course, there was also the suggestion of lifeguard training. They renamed the hall Lake Rochester. I always wanted to have something named after me.

Fortunately, time passed, and my faux pas was no longer the talk of the dorm. What works well for humanity is that someone else will screw up more than you did. Before long, the new topic is someone else's error or oversight. Of course, alcohol is involved in most of the missteps on college campuses.

Same dorm room, same year. I had a roommate who was a mischievous MacGyver. I'll call him "Tony." I hesitate to share some of his exploits because I am unsure of the statute of limitations on his verging-on-criminal undertakings. He never meant ill to anyone, but boy, did he have a great imagination. It worked well for his business. Nevertheless, when set free, an overactive imagination can lead to harrowing results in college. I came back from somewhere, but I can't recall where, to find Tony blissfully engaged in his project. His newest experiment was in full production mode. Yes, he decided to build a swimming pool in our communal showers. Back then, showers were taken in a locker room-style setting. Or was it prison style? It was a half-dozen nozzles that poured down, spaced three feet apart. Privacy was not an option.

So, Tony's great idea involved a few steps. First, he took down the toilet partitions in the bathroom and installed them on the inside wall of the 12' by 25' shower. Then, I believe he used toilet paper to seal the joints — an interesting use of toilet paper that the manufacturers never advertised. But miraculously, it worked. When I arrived at the scene, all the shower heads were blasting, and three feet of water had been collected thus far. He proudly stated, "Get ready for the pool party!"

This was a brilliant idea because we could envision a steady flow of girls flocking to our dorm on a Saturday night, wearing bikinis or less. Tony let the water rise to about four feet and declared, "Mission accomplished!" We managed to try out the new use of our shower room, splashing and laughing. Everything was going well until someone from the floor below came running up in a panic, saying the ceiling beneath us was collapsing.

Turns out water is kind of "heavy" - 64.2 pounds per cubic foot, to be exact. Tony had potentially introduced 1,200 cubic feet of water to the shower floor - over 30 tons. My resourceful roommate pried the petitions off the wall. The deluge of water flooded the bathroom and spilled out into the hallway. Once again, our neighbors were greeted by a squishy carpet. It was an away football weekend, but still, a few people remained in the dorm.

I felt confident we wouldn't be thrown out of school for an accidental mess. But this was a premeditated, mischievous idea executed by my roommate and me. It could have some serious consequences. I didn't know the punishment for being an accomplice in this attempt to create a girl magnet. Somehow, we escaped unscathed. By this time, our mates were accustomed to a waterlogged dorm, and I felt the relief of hearing that my parents had not been called, asking them to pick me up from the school that had expelled me.

Water-inspired events have given me far more stories than one has time to read, ranging from skiing on a lake near where I grew up to riding the waves at the beach. I wish they had an Olympic competition for body surfing. I would've dubbed myself a serious contender in the wave-riding event. Of course, I would have been out there competing against a bunch of 10-year-olds.

Nuts & Bolts: When considering the short term, keep your head down after an embarrassing moment. The goal is to move forward. Help is on the way. There's another dumb ass coming up just behind you, and the focus will change.

Considering the broader perspective, a creative imagination can be a tremendous asset to your career, so hang in there during the early explorations. Make a splash and enjoy!

Story 2
It's Better With Your Clothes On

I remember a moment when I decided to put a certain theory to the test—clothes or no clothes? If you trust me, I can save you the effort (and embarrassment) of testing this yourself. Imagine me as a freshman in college at Clemson. It's just a week into campus life, fresh off the Lake Rochester event. It didn't take long to realize that my high school letterman jacket didn't carry much weight on campus. In fact, nothing I brought with me held much clout. That's the reality of being the new kid—no one asked me about my high school accolades. I quickly learned that the past didn't matter here. It taught me right away that I had to put it behind me and start earning the respect of my new peers.

I lived in Johnstone C-5 with a resident assistant, whom I will call Steve to protect his anonymity, who was a Senior. Steve's role was to oversee a bunch of freedom-drunk newbies looking for firewater. Steve was a good guy, not one of those nosy types snooping round the rooms for a reason to get us in trouble. And I'm sure the pay was not all that desirable. Considering everything, Clemson probably should have hired a police force to keep us in line instead of an easy-going upperclassman.

During the first week on campus, Steve reminisced about the good ole days when he was in college circa 1973. In his era, one of the most popular college events of the year was streaking. Pretty self-explanatory. Yes, you remove your clothes, except for your shoes, because you must protect your feet. Other streakers join you, then you run around in public hoping to shock some anonymous bystanders and ultimately solicit lots of laughter. I recommend not doing this in your hometown unless you want those innocent victims to be able to identify you in a police lineup in your birthday suit. For some reason, campus law enforcement turned a blind eye to this activity. I suppose it was because we were considered young and foolish, and they were in some way protecting us from our own poor judgment.

Steve decided it might be appropriate to relive this nostalgic pastime. We talked about the fact that this fad lost popularity a couple of years ago. It went the way of the panty raid, which never made sense. I couldn't understand the idea of shouting at girls' dorms to persuade them to toss down an old pair of underwear.

After some rounds of customary firewater shared around the campfire, our idea began to gain momentum. Why don't we make a trip around the girls' dorm tonight? It was reminiscent of a dream I've had in which I am wandering around in public with no clothes on, and it doesn't bother anybody. When I snap awake, it feels so real that I have to take a minute to convince myself it never happened. This discussion around the campfire became so much like a dream that I couldn't tell if this idea was really happening.

Well, the streak was on. It was led by a guy who should have known better, Steve. My roommate and I were in. What can I say – peer pressure got the best of us. We ended up with about a dozen participants – enough for a football team with a substitute if needed. And enough to be somewhat anonymous if we ran fast enough.

A couple of hours later, I showed up at the meeting spot wearing gym shorts—just in case. I needed to be sure Steve wasn't joking. To my relief, Steve and the rest of the crew showed up in gym shorts too—Plan B, in case Plan A didn't pan out. I let out a quiet sigh, followed by a reassuring thought: This is exactly why I chose this school—plenty of smart, cautious classmates. Once we were gathered en masse, we found our courage, took orders to fall out – which is Army slang for 'Let's Get Going'– and followed the final command: Drop your drawers. We did it!

The first hundred yards were fun. Although it was dark, bystanders could see we were naked as jaybirds and gave some encouraging shouts. We were hooping and hollering, feeling young and carefree. College campuses are much more open-minded than the folks on Main Street. Following our new leader, General Steve, we turned the corner by the girls' dorm. Suddenly, lights flashed at us from every direction. We went from being the icons of freedom into cat burglars caught in the act, except that we didn't have any tools. Little did we know that one of our new dorm mates was a drama club member who had set up a makeshift stage with lights. Did I mention we were streaking past the girls' dorms?

We were trapped. Our battalion came to an abrupt halt when we realized that Mr. Drama Club had called all the girls' dorms to notify them of the spectacle about to unfold. And they wanted to see it. We heard cheers. I don't think there was any laughter, so I'll stick with cheers. There must have been more spectators than at my high school football games. Our anonymity was stripped away because, wow, those lights were bright. Really bright. The mischievous Mr. Drama Club, who ruined a perfectly good streaking night, also brought a microphone for a little color commentary.

I remember it as if it were yesterday: "Tom Rochester" shouted over the speakers, followed by a big cheer from the crowd. I didn't even have to score a touchdown to earn that cheer.

At that moment, as I struggled to find cover, I was considering what school to transfer to the next morning. My legs felt pretty rubbery, but the group was motivated to keep running instead of stopping for a formal review—until we heard Mr. Security Guard blow his whistle and shout for us to halt. Like a bunch of drunks sobering up quickly, college kids usually follow those orders. Not this time—we took off running quickly, adding insult to injury. If you could visualize what those security guards looked like, you could imagine they were no match for streakers. We were in the prime of our young lives, and many of them had physiques like the Penguin in Batman. Plus, we were pretty motivated not to be caught naked. I did manage to hold my gym shorts in my hand this entire time. Though not a survival kit, they saved me once I could no longer hear the whistle, for I stopped long enough to pull my shorts up to my waist. Then, I jogged as if I were just out for some exercise. This had started to feel like one of those dreams I mentioned, except this really happened. Or did it?

Fortunately, my fellow sprinters all escaped the long arm of the campus law, which I guess had pretty short arms. We reconvened at the dorms to discuss our harrowing experience. We plotted to prank our turncoat Drama Club neighbor. He apologized profusely, but it didn't work; he's probably still scared to this day. Although we were shaken and disappointed, we were able to identify a few bright spots: none of us got caught, and the girls cheered. Win-win. No boos, as I recall, but no phone numbers either.

In retrospect, this was the beginning of a camaraderie that continued for years. We showed up, naked, yes, but we also showed up willing to take risks, have fun, and do this crazy thing together. We were still enrolled in school in the morning. I decided to retract my mental applications for transfer.

Nuts & Bolts: I hope you laughed a little at my experience. We look better when clothes are on. I considered who came up with the idea of wearing clothes in the first place. I'm glad they did. I don't aspire to go around with big leaves covering my private parts—too much exposure.

Exposure can feel like a toxic word. It's often linked to everything from sunburns to nuclear radiation. It's much worse than running around naked. Another way to think about exposure is an opportunity to be your true self. Let others see that you are not perfect. It may feel awkward at times. Exposing ourselves can be uncomfortable. But who we are needs to shine through.

Story 3
One Shovel

My roommate, Tony, thought it would be a fantastic idea to leave the friendly confines of our dorms and move into a dilapidated trailer park on the lake. I was now a junior at Clemson, and Tony and I decided it was time to grow up and move off campus. I let him take the lead. To understand his decision, you must know that Tony was an excellent water skier. In fact, he traveled to tournaments with the college ski team. No scholarships accompanied the hobby, but it required a lot of athletic skill to compete. Running a slalom course, trick skiing, and jumping were the events, as I recall. I was a competent skier but not good enough to give up my weekends, especially when I had a perfectly good campus to enjoy as I sought female companionship. And that was my goal!

There was a lake beside the campus, and the ski club owned a great ski boat. Who cared where we were living– we could see the lake right out of one of our tiny windows! We committed to the trailer because it was so close to the boat parked at the dock. We had a vision of this setup as a girl magnet. It was a nice boat and a not-so-nice trailer. We had several visitors during the first month of school, but didn't anticipate the cool temperatures setting in and bikinis falling out of favor. The visitors stopped. We were in our single-wide, 1950s trailer, isolated from our peers on campus and surrounded by lint heads who worked at the local textile mill. "Lint heads" is not a derogatory term; it simply indicates that when your shift was over, your head was covered with lint—the result of running a weaving textile machine for eight hours. Our attire of old blue jeans and t-shirts showcasing rock stars made us appear like aliens in the trailer park. Somehow, we were tolerated.

I grew up in a blue-collar world myself. I had hoped a college education could help me climb the social ladder. I'm still not great at social niceties, but I know where the table's knives, forks, and spoons belong. I didn't need to take an etiquette class because I learned it by watching waiters set up tables while hanging around nice restaurants.

And boy, did I learn lessons while living in our trailer park. Guess how many shovels you need in a trailer park? The answer is one. Everything is understood to be shared. You don't even have to ask as long as you put it back. This philosophy clearly applies to property both outside and inside our home. I remember many times when a half dozen kids would sit on our couch watching TV, exploiting the fact that we had splurged on cable, while I assume the rest of the neighborhood had not. We would tell the children to go home, and they would beg to watch the end of some show. Depending on our mood, we might say yes before ushering them out the door. I don't remember our trailer having a working lock, so controlling entry and exit was not an option. Parents were just glad to have the kids out of their hair and never came looking for their missing children.

I wondered if our blue-collar neighbors would have wanted to know much of what we were brainwashed with in college. Many times, I questioned the value of some of the college courses. 1600 English literature and Medieval history didn't seem to apply to being a civil engineer. My trailer park neighbors, I am sure, wondered why a nice house had to be 5,000 square feet. Do we really need that much space? On the other hand, I've often wondered how folks manage privacy in a two-bedroom single-wide with four kids occupying the same space. I never mustered the courage to ask that question.

As much as I enjoyed my neighbors, I was miserable. I needed all the stars to align to find a female companion. My living situation wasn't helping. My roommate tried to give me a pep talk. Tony told me it wasn't all bad; our home was cheap. He didn't mention that it was dumpy, and we had to use our oven to assist with heating. That metal can should have been condemned as a fire hazard. I don't believe we had air conditioning, which probably wasn't a viable choice in 1950s trailer living. This semi-regrettable decision about our living situation created loneliness. I became disconnected from friends I used to see daily. Those relationships never re-established.

There was a bright spot late in my junior year: I met Cindy while at a local bar. The first time I took Cindy to my place, she didn't jump out of the car and run away as we drove down the pothole-filled road to questionable surroundings. I'm sure to the average bystander, it might have looked like a hostage-taking event. However, we did have a rotary dialing phone available for use in case of emergency, which probably made her feel more comfortable.

It was a great test. Even though Cindy knew I had the option of living in other upscale areas, she was obviously willing to be my companion through all varieties of lifestyles. I appreciate that she didn't view blue-collar living as something to be ashamed of, for we both grew up in modest environments. Neither of us lived in a trailer park, but we had friends who did. Anyone can seem special if driving a brand-new fancy car that forces you to lean one way because of a fat wallet. She looked beyond my current circumstances. She understood I was just another college kid, not defined by my parents' limited financial success. Although I would have liked to make a better impression on our first date, considering my circumstances were similar to homesteading in the 1800s, I did accentuate the positive. We did have running water and no outhouse. Tony's plan wasn't completely bad after all.

My point is that Cindy overlooked my living situation for my incredibly good looks and my fancy way with words. She has been my wife for 42 years. I have remained impressed with her great taste in men. Lucky me. In retrospect, without this bad decision, I wouldn't have known what a good decision looks like. Would I have met my wife? Maybe. Maybe not. But I can say that this regrettable choice led to a surprising and wonderful consequence.

I learned a lot from living in a trailer park. I appreciated the company of hard-working people who were content to clock out after their shifts, come home to friendly neighbors, share food and stories, and live with a smile on their faces. They lived for the day, not for tomorrow. I don't plan on returning—not because it was terrible, but because I like where I live now. I'm grateful for the experience. It had its dysfunctions, but so do people residing in 5,000-square-foot houses. We are not what we live in. Unless we consider what is inside of us.

Nuts & Bolts: My takeaway is aimed at younger folks: look beyond the obvious regarding people and places. My wife had choices and made her own based on our chemistry and shared values. Too much time is spent pursuing what isn't essential, like superficial appearances and a degree. Education doesn't automatically make you a better person. My trailer park neighbors made a point that resonates still: there's no place like home, regardless of how it looks. Our surroundings do not define us – so what if your home has wheels? You won't even need your own shovel. However, I do recommend having a functioning lock on your door. You don't want any uninvited rugrats.

Story 4
The Hubris of Youth

I am a little embarrassed to tell this story. I suppose that if you are telling stories, you have to share some that you just as well wish you hadn't participated in. It involves driving under the influence. I wish I had been wiser. I will attempt to inject some humor in it, but please know I take this seriously. Drinking and driving is a serious offense. I hope no one else puts their lives at risk by being behind the wheel after having fun while drinking with friends. But I experienced a lesson in loyalty that has stuck with me for over forty years, so the story is worth telling.

An incident from college illustrates just one of my many missteps. It started as a lovely afternoon at the beach with many of my college friends. We dipped in the water, threw a frisbee, and, of course, drank beer late into the afternoon. It was sunshine and laughter, good friends and good fun. As the sun set, we piled into my car for the ride home. I was in the driver's seat with six passengers in a Toyota Celica. For those unfamiliar with this older model, it is slightly larger than a Smart car. It looked like an automobile stuffed with clowns. We had gone just a mile or two when a highway patrolman pulled me over.

Now, my fellow passengers had already decided I was getting a DUI and were pondering how they would get home, leaving me behind. Some friends! Betraying me in a time of need! Annoyed, I told my cramped and over-served companions to be quiet, and the conversation only stopped when the blue lights came on.

But there was one person who wasn't participating in the game of Survivor. There was only one young lady in the car, and she was sticking by my side. Instead of joining the crew in abandoning the ship, she vowed to stay with me even if I had to visit the local law enforcement facility. That impressed me.

The policeman asked me to get out of the car, which I did. He noticed that there weren't enough seat belts for my friends. I told the Officer, they were my former friends. That I was just doing the Good Samaritan thing by taking them home, even though I was tempted to leave them behind forever. *Note*: I suggest avoiding this dialogue with a police officer. He wasn't concerned about how my car crew was getting home, but about my driving skills.

He took my license and registration and went back to his car. Meanwhile, my heart was pounding in my chest. This would not go well when I went home to see my parents. It wouldn't look good on my resume either. The policeman came walking back to my over-stuffed automobile. I remember noticing a big chew of tobacco in his jaw. He didn't look like one of those cops to show empathy.

He got about 6" from my nose. Still remember the stench of tobacco juice on his breath. I didn't comment on it, though- I hadn't completely lost all common sense. Turns out that the barometer for arrest was based on the remaining travel distance. When he asked me how far I had to go, I told him about a mile. This was 1979, and apparently, a mile was short enough to drive without getting hauled into the police station.

He said, "Son, let me tell you two things. One, I'd better never see you on the road like this again." Sounds fair, and I nodded in agreement. I was starting to breathe, for I could see I might get away instead of being hauled away. "Two, get rid of the beer right now." In a state of shock, I realized I was holding a beer. I responded by guzzling the beer as if he was challenging me, and I'm sure he was shocked, too. I was now in a delusional state. My friends thought I was bad-ass. I thought, Why did I do something so stupid?

Well, he was gone. So was I. Heading home- without a police escort. My former friends were now big fans, thinking it was really cool how I handled the situation with the cop. Guzzling a beer right in front of him was gutsy. I didn't respond; I was still trying to figure out how to get home without being stopped again. Guardian angel-like. I was very fortunate.

The young lady sitting beside me was not part of the abandon ship party. She was going to stay with me regardless of the trouble ahead. It is easier to leave someone in times of trouble, but it takes a lot of courage to stand with someone who is struggling. I learned a lot from that experience. First, my lady friend modeled what it means to be a friend in times of difficulty. Also, I realized the significance of being a designated driver. I must be capable of performing the task.

There are plenty of opportunities to stand by someone, even a stranger, when they have made a bad choice. We certainly should not ostracize those who make mistakes, but rather encourage them not to let what appears insurmountable define them.

As for the female passenger in the car, I married her three years after the incident. She has seen some challenging circumstances throughout the 40 years of our marriage. She is still loyal. As am I. I am lucky to have her.

Nuts & Bolts: Let's consider the word 'loyal.' Sure, everyone can be by your side when things are going well. It can be pretty lonely when the situation is not. So, when you have a friend who could use your friendship, run to it. Let's be better at running to problems. Even when it is someone you don't know, find a way to encourage them. We are all human, and we have all made bad decisions. Show up and care.

Story 5
Strike Three

So, I'm not good enough. That's the message I get when I'm rejected. Rejection is not pleasant. It squashes our immediate dreams. I remember living in our trailer when I was in college. My roommate and I decided to go to a concert in Spartanburg. I can't remember who was playing. But I know it wasn't The Who. My roommate had a steady girlfriend, so finding a date was not an issue for him. I, on the other hand, had some work to do. I recall being pretty cavalier about it. I was pretty confident this would be an easy enough task. So, I set out to find the girl lucky enough to accompany me.

Back then, everything was done face-to-face or by telephone—a rotary phone at that. It was not quite two cans connected by a string, but compared to today's technology, it might as well have been. Anyway, I could not text the invitation. I had to do it with words coming out of my mouth.

I got on the phone with Prospect #1. She was a girl I knew from an English class who had seemed to be interested in me. I was sure this would be a lay-up. For those non-basketball fans, it is a shot rarely missed. The conversation went like this: "Hey, this is Tom Rochester. How was your day? Did you have any luck with the paper we are supposed to write?" I hoped the conversation went well enough to get some gossip on the prospect's dorm floor. Eventually, I got around to asking the question, which sounded a little like, "What are you doing Friday night?"

Sounds presumptuous, don't you think? Thinking about it now, it sounds like I'm saying, if you are not busy, you would really be fortunate to go out with me. Well, she did not register that response. I hit the bottom of the rim. I must have misinterpreted her level of interest. Prospect number one gave me some mumbled excuse that told me not to bother anymore—unlucky girl.

I assumed Prospect #1 was an aberration. I would have better luck with Prospect #2. However, she indicated she had to go home for the weekend. It was an away football weekend that fall day, which meant it was easier to let a date off easily, as hard as I was trying to sell myself. "I am going home for the weekend" sounds acceptable. She probably immediately started looking for transportation home. #3 said she had a boyfriend. How was I supposed to know who was out of the dating pool? It's unlike today, when you can look at Facebook to see someone's dating status. Maybe it was #4 who shared with me that she was married. At 20 years old, I did not know you were supposed to be looking at girls' fingers.

At this point, I believe I may have better luck with in-person invitations rather than phone calls. I assumed it was harder for a woman to turn someone down when the guy was standing before her. It would catch her off guard, and she could not look at the list of excuses taped to her dorm wall beside the telephone. However, my theory proved wrong, and the in-person encounters didn't improve. I recall I had eight rejection experiences. My poor roommate, who had to listen to the results of all my feeble attempts, was wincing after watching me receive each rejection and probably considered looking for another roommate.

My roommate was now ready to throw the Hail Mary, a football term used in desperation when everything else has failed. Typically, it ends with a bad outcome. So did this attempt. My roommate's girlfriend, trying to be helpful, offered to set me up with a friend who had a good personality. My ego wasn't about to accept this overture. Well, the clock ran out. A term used in every sporting event, meaning time is up. Game over.

I was rejected, and didn't end up going. I felt a little lonely. I can't remember what I did, but I typically would catch up with some friends on a barstool somewhere. By Monday morning, I had restored my bruised ego. Enough so that when I went to a bar with friends a month later, I had the courage to ask this attractive coed, Cindy, to dance, followed by an invitation to a dinner date. (She is sitting on the couch next to me as I write!) I had the courage because I had survived eight rejections – so what if it was nine! Now, I get to laugh about my many rejections because Cindy has been my incredible companion for over 40 years.

What would my life look like if I had never been told no? I would have ended up in a completely different place. So what if I made a dozen phone calls that led nowhere? I regrouped and continued to grow from the rejection. I learned to dust off my uniform and got back on the playing field. I love Winston Churchill's definition of success. "Success is moving from one failure to another with no loss of enthusiasm." Words to live by.

Nuts & Bolts: In many cases, hearing "no" is what ultimately drives us toward a "yes." Think back to your own rejections—whether it was a job interview, asking your Dad for a car, or getting cut from a team. Our initial response is often to view these moments as painful, unfair, or even life-altering. But rejection also builds resilience. It forces us back to the drawing board—an old expression for starting over or reevaluating what we once thought was flawless.

I'm not suggesting we actively seek out rejection as a way to grow stronger. Life will hand us plenty of it on its own. Still, we must challenge ourselves to the point of failure from time to time. Otherwise, how will we ever know where our true limits lie? Playing it safe may sound like a wise motto, but a life without risk—or rejection—can become quite ordinary. So, should we seek rejection? Not exactly. A better way to frame it might be: reach beyond your comfort zone, aim higher than what seems possible, and dare to imagine the unattainable.

CHAPTER 3

Stories about

Hanging the Shingle

&

Hitting the Road

Story 1
Just My Imagination

"It's just my imagination running away with me." Thank you, The Temptations, for that 1971 release. And, boy, do I got a great imagination. It's one of my strongest attributes. My ability to see things as I want them to be, not as they are in my worst fears, got me through one of the roughest times in my life. It was when I left a comfortable job as a construction product manager to start my own business, selling construction material.

My imagination showed itself early in life. In the 1st grade, I had a reading problem. There were letters on the page that other kids could figure out were words when I couldn't. But I had my imagination working overtime. When it was my turn to read, I saw those pictures of Dick and Jane and told an incredible story from what I imagined they were doing. The intellectuals around me—classmates who had no trouble reading- listened like I knew words on the page that were beyond their comprehension. The teacher recognized my inability to read and sent me to the Special Ed Lady. They didn't grade imagination on our report card. It would have been my only "A" in the first grade. Given the system in the early 60s, most of my fellow Special Ed students were destined to have their names on their shirts when they started work. I'm not being judgmental. That's the way it was back then, and people need to know that.

My mother did some exceptional things to keep me on a different track. The Special Ed Lady had a lot of other youngsters to attend to, so I learned to read from my Mom. She also taught me early on how to study. More importantly, she just kept encouraging me to hang in there. She told me I would figure it out. That is about all a 6-year-old can understand. Years later, she went to my sixth-grade teacher and asked if they would allow me to read with the overachievers. That was the tipping point: I felt I was in the company of peers who would have successful careers, and I could imagine myself belonging with them.

When I was 9 or 10, I realized that my imagination was a powerful tool in life. Seeing things the way I wanted them to turn out worked for me when I was playing Little League Baseball on the Sealtest team. Sealtest was the name of the local milk producer, and I don't believe we received free ice cream as part of the sponsorship. It didn't matter; we kids only cared about whose Mom brought the snacks after the game—none of that store-bought stuff. Chocolate fudge was my favorite. My Mom made the best. You could tell by looking at me in the team pictures that I'd eaten a lot of chocolate fudge.

Baseball didn't come naturally to me. In fact, I went the whole season without a hit. I don't think I ever swung at a pitch. I relied on a walk every time I stepped up to the plate. Fortunately, it happened often enough that my teammates didn't notice. My Dad did. He wanted to change my baseball future.

He sat me down. This wasn't a talk regarding the birds and the bees. It was way more important than that. He never told me how bees were made anyway, and I don't blame him. We were there to talk baseball. He had done a little research. He told me to visualize the pitcher throwing the ball and then picture myself swinging the bat. I was to watch in my mind as I made great contact with the ball, and it sailed over the outfielder's head. I was to visualize heading to first base and beyond. I could see the crowd go wild- probably a half-dozen parents screaming. This vital lecture aimed to get me out of my slump. Well, I took his advice to heart. Dad taught me how to apply my imagination to achieve my desired outcome.

I entered the next season with some confidence, which led to a bit of success that built even more confidence and ultimately resulted in my selection for the All-Star team. Back then, they didn't record statistics, but if anyone remembers, I was the best hitter on the team. There was a game against Farm Bureau, our arch-rival. I hit a ball over the shortstop into the gap between the left and center fielders, allowing me to run all the way around the bases. For a chubby kid to make it all the way around, that had to be a well-struck ball. I don't recall who else was on base, but I do remember we won the game. I think I got an extra brownie from the team mother for my gallant effort. The following year, I made the All-Star team!

I needed my powers of imagination when I was 25 and decided to hang out my own shingle. Starting my own business was my way of saying to the world, "I am leaving my comfortable place in the workforce and striking out on my own." The first day on my own felt pretty good. Shortly thereafter, however, it started tumbling down. Business development is time-consuming. Results are not immediate. There was a lot of risk and a lot at stake. I was afraid I would fail.

I came home many nights bewildered, for the reality was bleak, but I imagined it would somehow work out. My way of coping with the real world was to create an artificial one, in which I visualized success I hadn't yet achieved. However, you don't want to get carried away, for delusion can become a permanent state of imagination. Sooner or later, reality reasserts itself to expose our false perceptions.

However, sometimes your imagination can help you get over what feels like an insurmountable hump. There was a day when I had to attend a meeting that could create a financial mess. I worried about it all night, which, as we all know, will get you nowhere. But then, instead of letting my thoughts drift to adverse outcomes, I imagined a scenario that would enable me to close a significant project, which would alter the direction of the profit and loss statement. Somehow, just imagining a big sale made me feel better. And that day happened when I sold a metal ceiling system, which was the largest ever received by the factory. I swaggered then. Of course, I have imagined I am a rock star, but that will never happen. I guess we can't let our imagination get too carried away.

Nuts & Bolts: The world can appear to be a pretty scary place, especially when one has a limited understanding of the problems. Imagining things as you want them can lead to a better outcome. Why do I believe this? I have to, because I have children and grandchildren. However, it will require some effort to see the world differently. I'm gonna step up, and I will need a little help from my friends — and their friends. John Lennon had it right: "Imagine all the people living life in peace."

Story 2
Talent & Misery

By high school, I was playing baseball and football and had shot up a foot in height, but had not put on a lot of weight. It was in my senior year at a small high school in South Carolina. How could a 145-pound buck-naked, wanna-be superstar like me ever have an athletic career? Well, hustle was my true talent. I was slow, pretty skinny, and not very strong—kind of like a mosquito on the playing field, just annoying. But I would hustle. I had a great attitude and was reasonably intelligent, a trait that could be debated. It's interesting how sometimes the most talented individuals lack leadership skills, but that was beneficial for me. I didn't mind taking the lead.

I had an experience at the athletic banquet that illustrated my point. I'm not even sure if they still have those. Back then, it was expected that you'd bring a date. Athletic banquets and dating—well, that shows my age. There were no mobile phones back then, either. How did we manage? The banquet was held in the cafeteria of the elementary school I had attended because they had a stage. It included dinner —a little better than what we would get for school lunches —and had a speaker from the South Carolina college football team. He was not well prepared, as I recall. I had a date, Lyn, who was a friend throughout my high school career. We dated without expectations. She was nice company.

At my banquet, the coaches for each sport took turns discussing their team's successes. Our band performed significantly better than our athletic teams against their competition. Is band a sport? All those who were in the band thought the only reason people came to the football games was to watch them at halftime. They must have had a great director. They even had their own banquet. I played baseball and football. Again, not much talent is required. No tryouts, just show-ups.

My football coach, whom I liked a lot, started droning on about our six-and-four season. No state championship here. Suddenly, he stopped and said, "Rochester, stand up." He startled me. I thought I was getting busted for talking to my date, but I honored his request. He addressed the crowd of 100 attendees, which included parents, and said, "That Tom Rochester is one of the least talented players on our team." Then he paused. I couldn't tell if he forgot what he was saying or if he was finished. It got a little awkward. My date was probably eyeing the room for a ride home. Then he said, "But I wish I had ten more just like him." (For those who don't play football, it takes eleven men to take the field.) It was the hustle! He appreciated me for my attitude.

I felt relieved that he had come to his senses. Kind of. I still pondered his attempt at complimenting me. Nobody else considered it to be a transformative moment, but it's something I never forgot. I don't have talent when it comes to football, but hustle served me then, and it has served me well my entire life. I've found many things in life where I lacked talent yet still managed to succeed.

Speaking was a genuine challenge for me. I was worse than Moses, who was so frightened at speaking that he would have Aaron speak for him. I hadn't been spoken to by a burning bush either. Frankly, I was terrified of public speaking. I remember my lowest point in college when I signed up for a public speaking course. There was a really cute girl in my class, and I wanted to make a good impression on her. I hope she reads this so she might believe I've overcome my phobia. My first attempt was disastrous, and I ended up dropping the course. I was so nervous that everyone could see how anxious I was. I could see on their faces how concerned they were. They were struggling with me to get through the 3 ½ minutes because they recognized how much pain I was suffering. I started reading it too quickly, just to get it over with. My body language said it all. I was not meant to be a public speaker. I'm embarrassed to put this failure on paper. But wait, there's more.

I decided to tackle this fear head-on. I went to a speaking coach as a working adult. And was determined. I learned a great deal, including some key techniques. Politicians are particularly skilled in these areas. What I discovered, most importantly, is that to get better, you have to practice. Then, you have to get on the playing field. I mean the speaking playing field. Volunteer. Sunday school classes, business environments, and community activities. Raise your hand and volunteer. Most people won't, but they also won't become great speakers.

In my first job, during my second year, I had the opportunity to teach a class for all salespeople across the country. I can't say that I raised my hand, but I drew the short straw and was responsible for educating the sales team about our product. After many sleepless nights leading up to that day, I worried about repeating my terrible classroom experience at college. I remember when the MC called my name; it felt like an out-of-body experience. I walked up to the front of the auditorium and looked out at 100 of my colleagues, most of whom were senior to me, and it just clicked. The words flowed out, hands raised for questions, and I even got a few laughs as I went through my presentation. I finished to loud applause and realized it wasn't as frightening as I had imagined. I wish I could get my sleepless nights back.

Imagine you're standing on the high dive for the first time. You've watched other kids dive and then climb out of the pool. You think to yourself, that won't be me. I won't have the same experience. Well, in that vein, I had decided years ago that I was to avoid standing in front of people for the rest of my life. Everything changed once I took on this speaking engagement. That's when I realized I could excel at this!

Nuts & Bolts: I overcame circumstances I thought were impossible. I never thought my mind could make it work. It's like a good golf swing. You must be relaxed; otherwise, your performance will not be good. However, let's not forget that hustle and effort help the cause! Determination can outperform even the most talented.

Story 3
Check Your Luggage

I haphazardly started my own business with an ambiguous plan. Anxiety kept me up at night because, on some level, I knew my business plan had flaws. Three key factors enabled me to leverage my shortcomings and create success. The first was the willingness to do whatever it takes, which was the main ingredient to my progress. When I started my company, I simply walked off the end of the plank by leaving a good job that had me moving into middle management with US Gypsum Company. At the ripe old age of 24, I jumped into starting my own business with no understanding of what was below. You have to understand, 40 years ago, research was not easy. It was typically limited to a set of encyclopedias. To figure out the rules, you had to get on the dance floor and move. I didn't start with any clients. I took a leap of faith and moved from Dallas, Texas, to Charlotte, North Carolina, just to start my own business. It was a good decision because the Carolinas are a great work environment. Lots of growing companies here. But I just did not understand how business was conducted. How do you process orders? How do you do accounting? Eventually, I figured it out, but with no help from Google.

The second thing I identify as a key attribute to my success is good fortune. One of my first calls resulted in a huge order. It was the first week on the job, and I multiplied the commission by 52. I figured I would be rich soon! It didn't happen that way. I have a CEO friend who retired at the top of the ladder in a huge manufacturing business. Big ladder. He told me that anyone who does not say good fortune when discussing his career is lying. Probably so. Those who give a different answer could have a short

52

memory. But business success is not usually a hit-the-lottery experience. There are a lot of little decisions along the way, and a lot of helping hands.

You learn a lot from the potholes in life. I like the comparison of potholes to life's unexpected outcomes. A lot of times, you are past them before you realize how bumpy the road has been. Other times, you hit the brakes and avoid them. Or your engagement with potholes causes a flat tire. In my work world, a pothole could look like we gave the order to someone else, the order was canceled, or worse, we can't pay you yet. I had way more helping hands than holes in the proverbial road to success. My clients were rooting for me and sometimes doing work on my behalf. A client told me it was hard to be mad at me. I guess that was a compliment. And it's mostly luck, like the fact that we had a robust economy at this time.

I started my business in 1985, selling construction materials. This was a long time ago, in the era of corded telephones, Windows 1.0, which ran on top of MS-DOS, and bad music. The latter might be a slip, for the same case could be made about my '70s music. But 1985 was just a long time ago. I had to work hard to make up for my lack of planning. I suppose I learned a valuable lesson from my Dad and his lack of taking time for vacations. I worked too hard. I was always gone from home, building relationships with potential clients. I had to be at the right place at the right time. Thus, I had to be in many places. Not behind my desk. Hitting the road. A lot.

The third key to my success was my supportive wife. Not just encouraging, I mean supportive. I wasn't making any money for the first three years of my business. She had to work hard and become the breadwinner. Cindy was involved with a temporary labor service startup. On the weekends, she also cleaned and wallpapered apartments. Our schedules didn't overlap very often—an actual test of marriage. We would pass in the hallways, spend weekends under the same sheets sleeping, and then return to our respective occupations. Rinse and repeat. Again and again.

Typically, I spent four nights a week out of town. I arrived home after 8 pm on Fridays. On Friday night, I laid my cheap suitcase down. On Saturday, I headed to the office and returned home around 4 pm, making for a short day. One Saturday evening, I came home and noticed a look on my wife's face that suggested someone had died. As a concerned husband, I empathetically asked, "What's wrong?" By the age of 25, having been married for three years, I had become better at sounding empathetic. Her answer surprised me. She held up an earring and asked, "Where did this come from?" I think I answered non-sarcastically, "From a jewelry box, I assume." This was not the correct answer. It did not come out of her jewelry box but out of my suitcase. She was seeking a confession and hoping for an explanation. I was speechless, racking my brain to come up with an answer. It was like watching Jeopardy and not having a clue about how to respond.

Then it hit me. Two or three months prior, I had stopped by my parents' house, who lived four hours away. My Mom indicated that she had some gold earrings she no longer wore and thought Cindy would like them. Apparently, she put the jewelry in my cheap suitcase, where Cindy found them. That was not the answer my wife was expecting. I don't know if it was the delay or the weak presentation, but she was still ready to throw the book at me. She responded, "Great, now you're dragging your Mom into this." Maybe she thought I would call my Mom and ask her to cover for me.

A mother's intuition is uncannily strong. The telephone rang. My wife answered it. It was my Mom. After several cordial exchanges, she handed the phone to me. By doing this, she avoided dragging my Mom into any potential drama. Knowing my innocence, I wanted to stretch out the drama as long as possible. I heard Cindy in the background saying, "Ask her. Ask her!" Ignoring the request, I asked about my brother, my Dad, and anyone else I could think of. I heard Cindy say again, "Ask her." Then, sternly, she said, "ASK HER." I suppose it was time to end the suspense and reveal the truth.

I finally approached the subject and held the phone up so Cindy could hear. "Mom, do you remember putting something in my poor excuse for luggage a couple of months ago?" As Mom murmured, "Yes, of course, the earrings..." I could see the seething look on my beautiful wife's face begin to fade. Mom asked if she needed to speak to Cindy. I offered Cindy the phone, but there was no need for it. The explanation should have provided some relief. The moment was still awkward. Cindy was embarrassed for having accused me. I offered to take her to her favorite restaurant for dinner as a special treat. We quickly restored peace and harmony.

Nuts & Bolts: Is there a moral to the story? Yes! I understood the pressure of working hard to provide for your family. I realized that I had become obsessed and started to lose sight of the importance of my support team. I truly needed to stay connected to my wife in a meaningful way, even while working around the clock. Not just my wife, my family, and my friends. And when your Mom gives you earrings for your wife, remember to pass them along!

Story 4
A Good Night's Sleep

I got some good sleeping stories. Many occur outside of my home. I stayed in a lot of cheap hotels early in my business career. Since I was in the early stages of creating a business that sold construction materials, it was all I could afford at the time. I stayed at some Motel 6s, as well as decaying motor coach motels from the 1950s and 1960s that had never been updated. The least I ever paid for a room was $14.00 in 1986. I also had the option to pay by the hour. Opted for the all-night package. Alone. And I was frugal. But more importantly, broke. My business experiment had only a limited shelf life. I felt the pressure to create a cash flow in quick order.

I met some interesting folks along the way. I recall a few motel neighbors saying yes to the bed turn-down service. Those paper-thin walls would reveal the secrets from the other side. Sometimes it was porno movies, and other times, ladies attempting to reduce the amount of time necessary to get to another room. Sounded like they were pretty good at it. But it was impossible to sleep through the noises of the job.

Did I mention that I was broke? I remember one night when I had a big presentation the next day. I was going to attempt to get the architect, owner, and contractor to change the exterior skin of a building they were designing. A really tall order. It was important, and a lot was at stake for me. I needed a good night's sleep. And, wouldn't you know it, a couple of couples bought the all-night package. I guess it was cheaper that way—the all-night package with benefits—noisy ones. And honestly, it was an all-night affair. I considered banging on the wall, but that would seem impolite.

They might have been trying to conceive. On second thought, I should have made my presence known by turning the TV up as loud as possible to create some white noise. Still, I couldn't sleep.

The next day, a couple of cups of coffee got me through my well-rehearsed presentation. I think I got the work, but I can't remember. I was too tired.

Here's a funny story that wasn't funny at the time. I pulled into Greenville, South Carolina, without a reservation late at night. I had a bad habit of doing that. I started looking for a hotel or motel. Nothing was available. This was before the invention of VRBO, but I wouldn't have thought of it anyway. I finally found a Traveler brand hotel, which can be either of very poor quality or somewhat acceptable. This one was "contractor grade," and by this time, I could afford better. It was $95 a night. Oh well, with no other choice, I checked in. My wife would have slept in the car. I entered my room. In those cheap motels, you always try to decide whether it's better to sleep fully clothed on top of the comforter or between the sheets. I typically took my chances between the sheets and did a lot of hand washing.

At 12:47 AM, I remember a banging at the door. Someone yells, "Police! Open up." Damn! I holler, "Hold on, I gotta get my pants on." And I hear thump, thump, thump again. "Police, open up!" I don't know why I struggled to get my pants on in a time of crisis. You would have thought I had never stuck my legs in pants and pulled them up around my waist. And I returned the holler, "I'm coming. I'm coming." As I got to the door, I determined that the first responder didn't want me, but wanted my neighbor in the next room. I know this because the neighbor answered the door and started a conversation with the Police. I never opened my door, a bit worried that guns might be involved. I was in no mood to sleep after the interruption.

So, there I was, lying in bed, trying to get my heart rate down to just a mild heart attack level. An hour later, I heard another interruption, this time from the parking lot. I didn't expect a circus event to accompany my check-in. Out in the parking lot, through a window, I saw a woman beating a man with her fist. He had his jacket pulled over his head, which made it easier for her to assault him. If he had been beating her, I would have intervened. I wondered if that qualified as a form of discrimination. But I judged that he probably deserved what he was getting. He could have scammed this hard-working lady of the night. It might have been his wife who caught him with a temporary companion. I don't think it was a brother-sister event. Either a temporary or long-term arrangement was my conclusion. Although I never did ask them.

After being entertained for five minutes, the humane thing to do was to help this poor soul. Clearly, the other hotel guests felt he had not received adequate punishment. I called the front office and explained to the woman with a foreign accent that there had been an altercation in the parking lot. I hung up the phone, and the fighting ceased.

Finally, I managed to get a good hour of sleep. Then, my new best friend, who had a foreign accent, called and asked if I could fill out a police report. I began to wonder if I had a work competitor who was having way too much fun at my expense. I told her I must have had a bad dream. At that point, it was 5:30 am. I decided to take a quick shower and find a Starbucks. Much safer. I picked up that little sliver of soap and scrubbed. Once I was dressed and managed to put my pants on without a problem, I hopped out the door. I made sure to look both ways before exiting, though. And lived happily ever after.

Nuts & Bolts: One cause of sleep deprivation is worry. And I have been good at worrying. I have spent many hours with my mind racing about an undesirable scenario in life, most of which never come to pass. I have finally concluded that I have no control over others. This doesn't negate the seriousness of the problem, but worry doesn't solve it either. There is only one way to reduce worry: to turn it over to hands bigger than mine. And in this case, it is not a 7-foot-tall NBA player but rather the one who brought me here in the first place. If he is powerful enough to create me, he can address my worry. Submission is hard. I prefer to resolve issues myself. But you can't solve them all. Thus, get some sleep. Say the Serenity Prayer. "God, grant me the serenity to accept the things I cannot change, the courage to change the things I can, and the wisdom to know the difference." Sweet dreams.

Story 5
The Best of Intentions

I recently flew back from Dallas. I used to live there in the early '80s. It's funny how revisiting a place brings memories to the surface. It's like I would only remember this story because I was driving the same route. Well, my story here occurred on Pearl Harbor Day. Not that the day has any connection to it. It was a disastrous day for the United States. It's just that it was almost a downright devastating day for me on a very different scale, of course.

Back 40 years ago, I lived between Dallas and Fort Worth, in the Mid-Cities, as it was then known, near the Dallas-Fort Worth International Airport. I was taking my regular route to work. Pearl Harbor Day is December 7th   [this tidbit may come in handy while watching Jeopardy], which is how I know the very day my life almost blew up. I had a bad habit of driving without allowing my windshield to completely defrost. It gives you a very small view of the world outside as you peer through a six-inch-diameter segment of the glass. Just so you know, I am way more patient now and wait until I can see before I drive.

As I was driving then, I could see through the tiny portal in the frost-covered window a person walking down the road. As I got closer, I realized the person was a woman who appeared to be confused or distressed. Because I am a product of the South, and I was raised to look out for fellow humans in need, I stopped. I rolled down my window to ask if she needed help, and before I knew it, she was in the front seat.

Now that she was close, I could see that my new companion appeared to have had a long night out on the town. She was obviously still feeling the effect of it. But now I was her transportation to somewhere. But where? That I could not determine. When I inquired about where she needed to go, she looked at me like she had been beamed into the car from a different planet. Star Trek-like. I mentioned I was going to Dallas.

She perked up and repeated, "Dallas." Oh brother. This was meant to be a road assistance conversation and not a chauffeur situation. I then realized she had no clue what her final destination may be. Did I mention I was going to work? I was 24 years old, still very intent on proving myself worthy, and did not want to be late.

Well, it was too late to do anything but deal with my incoherent passenger. I pondered the worst-case scenario. Could I be charged with a crime? Would my wife believe this story? Can I avoid losing my marriage or reputation in this situation?

Well, my passenger began to drift off. She fell asleep right on my shoulder. Great. There she was, quite comfortable. Snoring every so lightly. Just then, I peered over to my left to see one of the ladies from my office waving at me. Can you imagine what she is thinking? And yes, she knows my wife and knows this woman on my shoulder is not my wife. My thoughts now drifted to losing my job and being charged with kidnapping. My wife started divorce proceedings. This episode would likely appear on the nightly news: "a promising young life, cut short by a supposed good deed." I smiled and waved back.

After about a half-hour ride going nowhere, I devised a plan to check this damsel in distress into a hotel—my treat, of course. I probably had a $200 limit on my credit card. I kept driving, trying to figure out how to do it. Should I carry her in, lay her down on the counter, and ask the check-in attendant about proper protocol in situations like this? My day was really getting messy.

I wanted to do the right thing. But I was struggling to figure out what the right thing would look like. I was wishing I were simply an innocent bystander to this almost-too-good-to-be-true story. I coasted off the Interstate, my new companion, of an unknown name, still comfortably slobbering on my shoulder. Then, I started to worry that a gastronomic event might be approaching soon, as I heard rumbling from my stomach. Boy, the thought of being safely behind my desk felt like a Christmas morning gift.

I pulled into the parking lot of a Ramada Inn, as I recall. I was sweating profusely. My comatose companion all of a sudden became conscious again—a miracle. I couldn't decide what to do. I was still leaning toward the idea of putting her in a room and hauling ass out of the parking lot. It turns out that the 30-minute nap did her good. She snapped off my shoulder, and the look on her face revealed she was pondering how the hell she had gotten there. I read her mind, explained that I found her on the side of the road, and offered her transportation home or wherever she might want to go. I was beginning to sound like a modern-day version of the Good Samaritan, but in my heart, I was wishing I were one of the characters who avoided getting involved.

Did I mention the day before that I had pulled up to a guy who had run out of gas? That goodwill encounter worked out great. I ran him to the station. Got a gas can. Took him back to his car, and voilà. Check the good deed for the day off the list.

This good deed was in the nightmare category. I assured my semi-conscious front seat passenger, no longer my shoulder rider, that I had done nothing but transport. No relationship took place. That didn't seem to bother her either way, quite honestly. I was relieved at that. But she started to comb her hair as if she were getting prepared for a meeting with someone who mattered. Instead of a hotel room, I offered my lunch money for the day. $10. This was before ATMs and cellphones. She took my generous offer. Opened the door and got out. Woo, that was close. It felt like I missed disaster by seconds and inches.

I went to my office assuming the worst again. I visualized the office assistant standing at the coffee pot, telling the story of Tom's new blond friend. I walked past her desk, avoiding eye contact, but quickly realized she was not acting any differently than on a typical day. I went to my office and set down my briefcase. I walked to the coffee pot and sensed there was no rumor floating around the office. All of my doomsday scenarios floated away, and I was safe for another day.

Nuts & Bolts: I am trying to conjure some takeaways. And there may not be! Some might think the takeaway is: "Don't try to help strangers." It is risky, true. But I disagree. Most encounters work out fine, and it's worth the risk. Still consider stopping when you can help others.

If nothing else, taking risks produces great stories! Maybe that woman could have been you at some point in your life. No easy answers, but I stick with the belief that caring is never the wrong step to take.

Story 6
Folly Beach

I'm standing in a convenience store and short-order restaurant, feeling pretty groovy. I love this place, a short drive away: Bert'son Folly Beach. There are six or eight folks in front of me. Finally, I ordered two bagels with everything and a fried egg on one of them. I stand aside and wait for my turn. All orders in front of me were filled. Then, the next half dozen behind me are also taken care of. I finally went to the counter and asked, "Do you have to put all the stuff on an everything bagel after ordering, or do they come that way?" The counter dude didn't understand my attempted humor. So, I tried again and asked, "Can you please check my order?" Berts is not all that organized. I knew that. There is no industrial engineering guy around here. My counter guy realized he'd overlooked my bagel order and apologized profusely. I smiled.

A big coffee pot is right out front, saying "free for anyone." Most people found at Folly Beach use their free coffee to buy a bunch of stuff. It's like a hippie throwback to the 1970s. It was a great era when music was at its best, and young people demanded to be heard.

I wanted to participate in the '70s revolution, but my parents thought it was a bad idea. You are judged as a participant in the revolution based on the length of your hair and how shabby you appear. Even Jesus was popular among the youth; after all, he was a revolutionary with his long hair, beard, and sandals—pretty cool. Unfortunately, my hair never touched my ears, and I looked pretty square back then.

Still looking a bit square, I smiled at the counter guy and said, It was fine. It was just a minor inconvenience. He added extra bacon to my bagel as a peace offering. I agree that bacon fixes everything. I left with my bagel, which had taken a 1/2 hour to secure, for the beach, sat in a chair, and watched the tide, in no hurry to go anywhere. I appreciated the scenery. I observed the women's bathing attire and decided we have watched the swimsuits dwindle to almost extinction in my lifetime. I might be too old to observe this, but the strings far outnumber the one-piece suits now, except for grandmothers. The counter guy had apologized, and that was good enough for me. Mission accomplished.

I realized, on this day, while eating a bagel by the beach, feeling the sun on my face, and the wind on my skin, that I have rushed through my life much too quickly and missed opportunities to have meaningful experiences. No regrets. I accomplished a lot. And now I am trying to reverse my race to the finish, but not by attempting to look younger. Truthfully, I do that, too. My attempt here is to let others know there is no magical finish line. High speed doesn't get you to your final resting place more efficiently than a modest pace.

These thoughts bring to mind a recent trip Cindy and I took to Vietnam, which was not like a short drive. It was 35 hours of travel. I do not want to discourage travel to Vietnam, for it was a great trip. It's just a long way away. Upon our return home, we found a 12-hour time difference between the United States and Vietnam. We were exhausted from sitting on an airplane. I never thought sitting could wear you out. Airplane food wore me down as well. I don't know why airlines feel the need to put something in front of me that is only slightly edible. Bert's would have been a big hit on the plane.

Cindy and I arrived home and realized we were back a day early because of the time zone change. It's a bit challenging to explain, as I struggle to understand it myself. The outcome, however, was that we were home and recognized we had an entire day with no crammed chores, errands, recreational activities, or social outings. This has never happened before—24 hours of unaccounted for time. What would we do with this newfound gift?

I have experienced the opposite, exceeding capacity, for most of my life. Generally, I have overbooked most of my days on this earth. For some reason, overbooking makes me feel more successful, more important. I even had to call audibles at the line of scrimmage. For those who aren't football fans, this means realizing at the last second that your plans won't work out. This quick adjustment is necessary because I have too much on my plate. I've been accused of holding back on commitments until I see if there are better options. I admit this is partially true.

There are a couple of philosophers worth mentioning at this point. I love Aesop's fable about the tortoise and the hare. I wish I had met Aesop. The guy told great stories and showed a lot of wisdom. Then there's Simon and Garfunkel, "Feeling Groovy." Regardless of our irrational pace, we have somehow forgotten how to live. "Slow down, you move too fast, you've got to make the moment last." Today, I am stopping- I don't mean I am throwing in the towel. I'm just going to sit on my rear end for a little bit here on the beach; listen to voices and other sounds; feel the elements; watch thoughts come and go in my mind. Of course, I'm going to eat my other bagel first.

So, what did Cindy and I do with our newfound gain? In this case, we enjoyed a leisurely breakfast, followed by a stop at an equestrian store that was off the beaten path. This was Cindy's choice, and it would have never taken me off the beaten track. We stayed on two-lane roads we had never enjoyed, passing through small South Carolina towns we wouldn't have visited with our usual, over full schedules. We engaged in a conversation that didn't include what we needed to accomplish that day.

After many years, I've changed my mind about having more to do than time to do it. I need extra capacity. Why? Because getting more done doesn't necessarily make one feel content. Instead, it's more important to be available to people.

When I am available, it means I have time to talk. I have time to help. I'd like to hear about your experience with an overloaded Instagram, Twitter, and Facebook world. (I keep these three social media distractions off my list to increase my capacity.) Keeping my time free has allowed me to think more clearly. Doing is not a substitute for reflecting. When you reflect on life, you have the opportunity to evaluate your priorities. For example, you realize you only live once, and you need to accomplish things that matter, like eating anything chocolate. I'm only thinking about it now, not doing it. But since I've written about it, I'll get an ice cream cone. I will take a grandchild with me so that I can call it a family outing. That is an example of using my extra capacity to focus on what's important.

Nuts & Bolts: I have learned to take a deep breath and say, "Wow, what a day!" I've learned what brings me joy. I like friends more than accomplishments. Learning something new. Pondering what this short time together is all about. I like the idea that this lost bagel order could start a trend. It could be a reminder to have a more fulfilling life by slowing down. Is it a folly to sit at the beach eating a bagel? Or is it the point?

CHAPTER 4

Under One Roof

Stories on Parenting & Marriage

Story 1
Someone Has To Do It

One fall day, a few years ago, I was driving through our community in the low country of South Carolina. Lying in the middle of the road was a dead raccoon. Seeing that dead raccoon on the road got me thinking about a heartwarming road-kill story--I know, an oxymoron. It involves my oldest son, Drew, on Thanksgiving Day, when Drew was about 23. We were driving down a two-lane back road, headed home from running errands, when the sun was just coming over the horizon. I don't think I'd finished a full cup of coffee yet. My mind was focused on what my Thanksgiving plate would look like. I was pretty excited, as I recall. Drew and I were on our way home when we passed a couple of mailboxes and noticed a woman standing by the side of the road, bending over a garbage bag. I was still wondering whether my turkey sits on mashed potatoes or beside it—a tricky question. Everyone needs to consider their dinner plate.

Drew's instincts kicked in, and he blurted out, "Dad, turn around." He interrupted my train of thought as I was considering my dessert choices. Still, I followed his directions. He had sensed something was wrong. We turned around and stopped beside a young woman wearing the gray Waffle House uniform with her name on it. We quickly learned that when she had arrived home, she had found her dog dead on the road, in numerous pieces, and she was crying. Drew didn't hesitate.

He scrambled out of the truck and started putting the pieces of the dog into the garbage bag. I was startled at first, but followed his lead even though I'm not great at blood and guts. It was nasty. I thought I was supposed to be setting the example, but Drew was way ahead of me, bag in hand, scooping and handling pieces of carcass with such grace. I, on the other hand, was losing my appetite.

Sidebar: Please take note. If there's a medical emergency, let's hope someone else is around. You won't want me trying to save the day. I held my nose, closed my eyes, and started scooping. I'm not good with blood and guts.

The young lady's first reaction was shock that someone had stopped. She even asked if we would charge her for helping with the cleanup. Drew reassured her we were there to help as neighbors and then asked if there was a shovel nearby. There wasn't. He told her he would be back. The dog deserved a decent burial.

Need I remind you it's Thanksgiving Day? At noon sharp, I plan to dive into the plate I've been designing. By 12:30, I'll be happily miserable, stuffed to the gills, and in need of a nap. Still, these thoughts didn't stop my son from thinking about how to help a stranger in a challenging situation.

On the other hand, when I was a kid, I was mostly concerned about fun. One of my favorite summer pastimes was cutting a bicycle tube in half and filling it with sand. I would tie the ends, and you would have a pretty convincing representation of a snake. Tie a long fishing line to one end, place it in the road, and head to the safety of a nearby ditch; then, you could slowly retrieve "the snake." You can convince many drivers moving at 40 to 50 mph that it's a real snake. The drivers would speed up and try to run over the reptile with both wheels. Unbeknownst to the snake haters, we were down in the ditch, pulling this piece of rubber across the road with the fishing line, leading to many good laughs. However, once everyone in the neighborhood figured out our little trick, its effect was lost. For a while, though, it was a good laugh.

Water balloons at cars were fun, but before you roll your eyes, just know that we never caused an accident. My mind would always wander back to the dead animals on the road and how much it bothered me. That's when I decided to invent a deflection device to warn animals of the dangers of the road. I didn't know what it would look like, how to build it, or if it would even work, but I was determined to find a way to stop critters from getting hit. Somehow, though, I feared the cause was probably hopeless. I must be honest; I feel bad when I hit an unsuspecting creature. However, I can't remember ever turning around to see if I could do something about it.

My son, on the other hand, wanted to take action. We get about a mile down the road, and I look over to see that Drew is obviously upset. Once again, Drew asks me to return to the crime scene. We do U-turn number two and pull up to the house, where the animal carcass is inside a black garbage bag. Drew steps out of the truck and opens his wallet. He pulls out $80 — every cent he has — and gives it to the young lady. All I have in my wallet is $2. I cough it up, but it feels disappointing compared to his gift. My son's actions clearly touch this woman; he must have been raised right. Good job, Mom.

We are now on the third attempt to drive down the road to get us home for dinner. Everything went smoothly, and I decided the mashed potatoes belonged on top of the turkey. Afterward, a good nap was in order, just as I had planned. As I napped, Drew fulfilled his promise and returned in the afternoon with a rusty shovel. He dug a decent hole for the dog and held a celebration of life for this deceased creature. I didn't ask if there were any attendees at the peaceful ceremony, but I'm sure my son did the dog justice.

The next morning, I heard gravel crunching in the driveway. In years past, I would have been hauling ass out the door to stop my mischievous child from sneaking out of the house. He's an adult now, I remind myself. I am not getting up anymore. To my surprise, he went to Waffle House to check on the dogless waitress. This is becoming increasingly unlike someone with my DNA. It was a proud moment, nonetheless. I never imagined looking at my son and seeing someone so much more compassionate than I had been at his age.

With Drew in mind, on that fall day in the low country, I returned to the spot where the sad raccoon victim had been lying in the road. Instead of driving by, I stopped and gave it a proper farewell. I didn't bury it, but I did place it in the nearby woods, and that felt like enough.

Nuts & Bolts: Who is responsible when something unpleasant happens? Are we a culture that simply shrugs and says, "Let someone else do it?" Whether it's removing a dead animal from the road or comforting a weeping stranger in public, do we take action, or do we let others handle the situation? Just remember, don't try to pick up road kill in oncoming traffic. That could cause issues I'd rather not address today. Seek opportunities that need attention and be that person.

Story 2
So You Want Perfect Kids?

One result of partnering with a fabulous companion is the arrival of a new human being on the planet. It is an amazing phenomenon that remains unexplained. Sure, scientifically, we understand the process of reproduction, but nothing touches the heart quite like the experience of a child being born. The concept of a human soul being introduced to our world is a miracle we often take for granted.

I experienced the birth of my offspring three times. I wish I could do it all over again. I have enjoyed watching my children have children, too. Nothing, though, can equal my first exposure to watching a human being emerge from my wife's womb. To be honest, I didn't see my daughter enter the world because I kept my eyes locked on my wife's agonized face. It's a good thing men don't have to go through childbirth. We are just not cut out for it.

Back to my first experience of a new life: My daughter was born. The gravity of the occurrence had not fully sunk in. I do remember feeling a brief panic that something wasn't right—did she have 10 fingers, 10 toes? I was relieved to discover that my fear was unfounded. She was perfect.

Babies aren't very attractive on day one. My Mom said all babies look like Winston Churchill. I don't think they look that good. But ours was so beautiful that I felt sorry for the other parents. I had never felt skin so soft; I couldn't stop touching it. And the body parts were so tiny—fingers and toes—so fragile. Yet there was a look in her eye, and I knew I was in for a lifetime of adventure.

There wasn't much dialogue apart from me making gurgling sounds. She occasionally made some inaudible sounds in response. Occasionally, an unexpected smile would spread across her face. It was a sign of a bowel movement, and that was fine by me. The nurses said it was time to go home, and I recalled my Dad saying he wished I had come with an instruction manual delivered with my birth. "Wait a minute," I said, "Where's the instruction manual for raising children?" She thought I was joking. I was dead serious.

I remember pushing my wife in a wheelchair out the front door with my daughter in her arms. I left her at the patient exit and went to get my car. After pulling up to load them into the vehicle, I realized I didn't know how to install a child's car seat in a vehicle. Fortunately, the nurse did. She had encountered one or two like me before.

I did master the skill of putting a child seat in a car before the next two were born. I experienced the same miracle with both of my boys when they became breathing members of our society. Then I wondered how to guide them as they journeyed through the rest of their lives. Conceiving and birthing them was the easy part. Now, how to shape them to have meaningful lives became a much bigger challenge.

So, the million-dollar question: How do we convert these potential juvenile delinquents into something society would approve of? Those perfect kids that we can showboat like a trophy case? I heard a piece of pragmatic advice years ago, and I'm sure it will be seen as old school. I attended a presentation by Zig Ziglar. For those unfamiliar with his name, he may have been one of the most positive individuals of his generation. He exuded positivity and authenticity. He didn't have to force himself to see the bright side; it just came naturally. Zig made a case for parents to increase their chances of having children who avoid the potential pitfalls of growing up. The list of derailments is extensive: bad grades, poor friendships, drug and alcohol issues, and even jail time. He asked the audience who wanted to enhance their likelihood of avoiding some of these regrettable outcomes. My hand shot up immediately—perhaps both hands. This was 40 years ago, and I was just starting to raise my child.

As a great speaker does, Zig paused. Remember to pause when speaking. Then he said, "Dads, go to church." It was that simple. I expected a more epiphany-like answer, perhaps something like sending them to military school. But no, it was simply: Dads attend church with the family. Why? If Dad plays golf, goes to work, or simply sleeps in, the children perceive faith-based activities as unimportant. Yes, Dad, you can daydream while the pastor makes the third point of his sermon. It doesn't matter if you absorb every lesson. The mere act of going conveys to kids that this is important. It's not foolproof—kids will be kids. Mine were. And so was I. This is code for the fact that I didn't always live up to my own expectations. Like all of us, I'm just living imperfectly.

My family was not particularly fond of church when I was growing up. We were Episcopalian. In our little town, the wealthy Episcopalians were the "haves" back then, while we were the "have-nots." Don't get me wrong; we were still "haves," just not in a monetary way. We had great values and parents who sought to bring out the best in their children. Eventually, my parents drifted away from the church.

Cindy and I decided to make church a priority. It's not the only way to connect with our maker, but it works for us. The kids, being kids, had to be incentivized, which meant a trip through the McDonald's drive-through on the way. We enjoyed eating lunch out after the service. Interestingly, later on, the kids indicated that they secretly liked going. They got to see friends in Sunday school and sometimes gained an interesting takeaway from a sermon. But on Sunday morning, we were going. It was non-negotiable. For us, it mattered. Cindy and I discovered that the church was a great place to make new friends when we moved to another unfamiliar area. It still is.

So, perfect children. Not a chance. However, if your goal is to help kids who will make the future better, care for others, and strive to surpass their parents' successes, then support them in leading a life of faith. And success is not a bigger house. It's just a contented one filled with those who act with love. It's way better than being the best player on the baseball team. My family tree is unlikely to produce anyone famous. We don't need to. We can do better than that. We can make people of character.

Nuts & Bolts: As I reflect on the moment when parenting became a reality on a perfect day in June in the late '80s, I hope all of humanity can experience a day of witnessing a miracle of life and remember to cherish it forever. Every child deserves to have caring adults waiting for them. Yes, the world is not perfect, but we need a culture that reveres parenting. My hope for today is that humanity will treat God's creations as unique and utterly valuable. It's better than exceptional; I just don't have a word for it. And we can all contribute, including with children who are not our own. The God who sent these incredible creations will be so pleased, and so will we all.

Story 3
Solving Lifelong Mysteries

Well, there are plenty of mysteries out there for me. For instance, how do we cultivate people of character, and how can a TV picture come through an electrical outlet? Or, when I look under a car hood, how do all these things work together to get me from one place to another? It's a miracle. The fact that some people have figured it out is amazing. I'll stick to understanding simple concepts: righty tighty, lefty loosey.

But here's a tough one for you: How do you understand the opposite sex in all her complexities? Many have said it's impossible. I have an idea, and I developed my theory by examining Playboy magazines during my younger years, and by reading The Five Love Languages later in life.

First, let's start with the basics. How does a young male understand the onset of hormones in relation to girls? One problem is that the internet has eliminated the need for imagination. Kids today can grasp sex education in five minutes on a computer screen, far more than I learned in the first eighteen years of my life. I'm okay with learning about women, as it was conveyed long ago, typically by older boys or through girlie magazines hidden under a friend's bed. As a result, I have excellent imagination skills.

When my older son, Drew, was around 12 years old, I attempted to explain the entire reproductive process. I felt it was my duty as a father to explain how men and women make children. We were in the car, so I had a captive audience. As I explained sex in detail, he squirmed like a pig. Of course, I shared the belief that you engage in this behavior when you are old enough to court a woman. I graded myself fairly well on the presentation. Reality set in when I realized he was staring at the door handle. He would have jumped out of that car going 70 miles an hour if he could have. I came to a screeching halt, not with the car but with my explanation. I asked if he had any questions. Looking solemn, he simply stated, "I won't tell Mama." I explained that Mom had a good understanding of the reproductive process.

Anyway, he returned from the 5th-grade class explaining that his teacher did a much better job of getting through this embarrassing subject than I did. So much for my teaching skills. I didn't even bother with my younger son. I've concluded that kids these days might be better off with professionals when it comes to hormones and courting gals. My advice on what to do once you settle down with a woman might be better.

I learned the secret about how to make a woman happy. No drum roll is necessary. The secret is to care for each other. That is a letdown for those of you anticipating something as significant as letting your spouse have full use of the remote control. While I was happily in love with my wife, I realized I needed another ingredient to make our relationship even better. It was care.

One way I learned about care was by watching my sons and son-in-law interact with their wives. My son-in-law was very attentive to my daughter's needs in a way that I wasn't with my wife. Both sons are very attentive to their wives' needs. I learned by watching. Care is a word that men can embrace. It is more of an action word, and I must admit that I overlooked it too often during my 40-plus years of marriage. Fortunately, I have an understanding wife. Cindy was quite self-sufficient. She knew I had to be committed to my occupation. I have thanked her many times for being a Mom and Dad. She indicated she wouldn't have it any other way.

It was my Dad who initially taught me about care. My Dad was a little chauvinistic early in my life. For example, he loved Archie

Bunker. That was a TV show depicting a lifestyle he appreciated. Not like he was ordering my Mom around. He just believed men had certain roles and women had theirs. Most families worked in defined roles before the women's liberation movement. I wasn't of age when women were burning their bras. Happened about the same time young men were burning their draft cards. I suppose there was a fascination with fire in the late 1960s. I'll write about the Woodstock era another time.

I am retracting my insinuation that Dad was a chauvinist. It implies he didn't appreciate women or my Mom. He cared a lot. It's just that men, like my Dad, wanted to appear as the ones who wore the britches in the house. However, everyone knew it was the wife/mother who was the most important cog in the wheel of making the family happen. She was the essence of the household. This story shows how much my Dad knew that and cared.

We lived in a rural part of South Carolina where education was not valued. I think our state was ranked second to Mississippi in having the poorest education system. Not a category to be proud of. My Mom had a dream of becoming a schoolteacher since she was a young girl. She married young and didn't actualize that hope. However, long before there were households with two working parents, Dad encouraged her. Then he cleared the way for her to go back to school. He assumed many domestic duties that men in those days weren't willing to tackle. My brother and I helped by taking on additional chores like washing dishes and washing clothes. We didn't have one of those fancy dishwashing marvels. I actually believe I can wash dishes in the sink as quickly as I can load the dishwasher and then unload it once the splashing stops. I used to get frustrated. Dad would say, "Tom, wash the dishes." Why me? Whoever was in my Dad's vision was assigned to the task, and I was often the visual target.

Bottom line- we stretched. Mom went to school a couple of nights a week and studied on the weekends. Dad took us to a cheap local diner once a week for dinner, and I liked that. Dad would supervise baths and put us to bed. Truth be known, we skipped some of the bathing activities when Mom was not there. Because my Dad was willing to do solo parenting with us, two young boys, in an era when that was not the norm, my Mom realized her dream. Mom became a school teacher. A lot of students benefited as well because she was an incredible instructor. I never had her as a teacher, and regret that I didn't. Dad cared for Mom and cared about what she wanted. He never did figure out how to make coffee. But Mom liked having an early morning to herself anyway. She always made the coffee.

She was more successful than my Dad in the financial world. It didn't change the dynamic of how they related to each other. Most men in the neighborhood would not have made such sacrifices to make this happen for their wives. Sacrifice means going to the back of the line, not begrudgingly, but with enthusiasm, and behaving selflessly, putting your priorities on hold. Dad did that. He showed me we can never care too much; it doesn't make you a doormat.

I recall a story about a man who had come to the conclusion that his marriage was over. He didn't feel appreciated, so he consulted an attorney to get advice on how to create a scenario with minimal financial damage. This still happens in real life. The attorney said, "Don't tell her anything yet. Just go home and wait on your future ex-wife hand and foot. It will set up a perfect exit opportunity when she sees how hard you tried to bring happiness."

The gentleman, who was looking forward to being single, followed the lawyer's instructions. A couple of months later, the divorce attorney remembered the meeting and called his soon-to-be divorced client. Asked him to come down and finish the paperwork. The gentleman happily responded, 'I don't need that paperwork anymore. You wouldn't believe how my wife acts like a different person.' Something to think about. Who really changed?

Nuts & Bolts: I still don't understand how WiFi works or what block chain is. And the mystery of sex education for children hitting puberty should be left to the professionals. But what about making women happy? That's more nuanced. As you contemplate your day, consider what care looks like and how it applies to your loved ones. Sometimes, care goes unnoticed. We all experience life without acknowledgment. Try assuming that your care was appreciated, even if no one made a big deal out of your effort – do it anyway. There will be times when your act of caring will have a big splash. Either way, believe and take the caring action. It will change your life.

Story 4
Don't Touch Anything

Those were my wife's words. She said, "I need to put you in a padded room." It was just after I tipped over a full glass of iced tea while we were eating lunch in our kitchen in South Carolina, sitting on our barstools. Funny that I met my wife on a barstool while at Clemson, and 45 years later, I still sit with this person - on a barstool. We eat meals sitting next to each other at the counter–no blaring music or nearby dance floor like the night we met. Now and then, we treat ourselves to something other than water that has a hint of kick. But we have both agreed to limit those occasions. Keep them special.

To repeat, Cindy told me, "I need to put you in a padded room." I agreed with my wife's assessment. As many mysteries as I have solved, I could not figure out how, in the prior 30 minutes, I had already broken the washing machine and the garbage disposal. To my credit, I did manage to fix the washing machine. I was a bit apprehensive about what might happen next, so I went and sat in my favorite chair to begin writing. I hadn't broken the pen yet, but my scribbling was just getting started.

While writing, I reflected on the fact that I have a wonderful life. A significant reason I have been blessed with one is that I partnered with the right spouse. I remember my Mom driving my brother and me to the nearby A&P grocery store when I was young. I always asked questions. I still do. Some were silly. They still are. I remember asking how Moms and Dads get together. There's no need to tell a five-year-old that lust and alcohol have a lot to do with it, like the night at the bar when Cindy and I met. Instead, she told me a story about God choosing one person on earth who would be a perfect match. I didn't ask her a follow-up question. Instead, I suggested getting M&M's at the grocery store instead of animal crackers. After all, I was growing up.

But I never outgrew my clumsiness. My ineptness is a combination of a lack of coordination and being in too much of a hurry. On some level, my tendency to rush should be rewarded. After all, I am trying to get more done. Overachieving. I considered the cost of this speedy approach. How many things had I broken? I couldn't make a list, but Cindy could. One thing I hadn't broken was my marriage. I tried to understand the mystery of why our relationship remained intact while others did not. I credit Cindy for most of the success. I believe that dancing with the one who chooses you helps to maintain monogamy. But often I had my priorities out of order, putting friends or work before my vow of "until death do us part' with my companion.

We started pretty meagerly. We both had a college education, but no actual possessions. My job took us 1,000 miles away just one week after we said, "I do." It might sound typical of the era of black-and-white TV, but it was pretty disruptive for us. However, looking back, we benefited from being taken out of our comfort zone. Cindy and I lived in a one-bedroom apartment in a blue-collar neighborhood. We did have a good apartment softball team, and I enjoyed spending Saturdays on the baseball diamond. One of our successes growing up together was having no one else to lean on—just a blank sheet of paper and a corded phone to reach out to our loved ones. Plane rides were out of the question, and we were on our own little island, except there were a lot of people around and no water. We did experience some homesickness. There's nothing wrong with missing our friends and family. We liked our old surroundings, but we eventually found our way. We met some of the best friends we've ever had. Making new friends when you have to start over is immensely gratifying—it made us feel accomplished.

Some of the best growing up was just starting as we raised our three children. Reflecting on episodes from our child-rearing years feels like a blur. There were harmonious moments alongside some disagreements, but there were plenty of funny times, too. My children may not remember my proudest achievements, but they can easily recount many of my blunders. It frustrates me when kids have such selective memories for disparaging stories. I worked a lot, and Cindy took on the roles of mother and wife, handling the essential tasks that kept our family running. Only recently have I learned how to use our household appliances, apart from the TV. We have so many modern conveniences, yet I still find myself putting dishes in the dishwasher, which I find really hard.

What I dislike even more is attempting to repair an appliance or any item beyond my skills; I often make multiple trips to Lowe's hardware store. I should buy stock in that company. I usually bring home every possible item that could help solve the problem. After several failed attempts, I watch YouTube, only to discover I should have bought some obscure tool that a typical customer wouldn't know about. I dislike following instructions even when I end up wasting a lot of time not doing so.

Upon closer examination, and without a marriage manual, good fortune played a significant role in the success of our marriage and family life. After all, we began as two strangers. Somehow, we chose to spend our entire lives together. Now that I think about it, it sounds risky, but it has worked out well.

Taking the time to understand my companion has been helpful. Notice I didn't brag about myself here. My brain may work differently from that of other human beings when it comes to listening and following directions. How can I keep my eyes fixed on my wife while thinking about so many different things? Work, the house, the kids, the dogs? How can I read a manual when I am convinced I know how to fix the garbage disposal? After all our years together, I am still confident that she doesn't know I'm watching the game while she's talking to me. Or that I am noticing a pretty woman walking by when I really should be focusing on her. Fortunately, I married someone filled with forgiveness. Okay, I am concentrating now. Seeking to understand is vital in all relationships. Sometimes you've got to suck it up and listen. Intently.

I appreciate my haphazard way of thinking and problem-solving. I wish more things in life were designed with me in mind so I could safely touch more stuff. How do you even break a washing machine? I think my timing was off. I just happened to be nearby when a light indicated that the door wouldn't open.

Sidebar: to rationalize the consequences of this broken washing machine. I didn't need to wear those clothes anyway, until the repairman showed up. At least I didn't have any ink pens in my pants. Well, is that true? Let's just wait until the repair technician arrives. He may also have some suggestions for removing ink. This may end with my wife getting a new wardrobe. I'll just wear my shirts with black ink spots and act like they came that way. I'll create a new fashion statement, like torn pants. I still can't figure out how holey pants became popular. This is how my mind works!

Some would say the best years are behind you after 45 years spent sharing the same arrangement on barstools. I don't believe that is the case for us. Sure, sex and alcohol have long ceased to be the reasons we hang out together. I don't think those two experiences are negative—they become less important over time. Now, I look forward to the conversations we share that I hope will never end.

I have done very little to unravel the mystery of matrimony. Or perhaps I have. Can any two people stand at the altar and experience a happy forever? Expectations should be both high and low. There's no need to assume your economic situation will include yachts and airplanes unless you're born into that lifestyle or hit the lottery. Most of us will never know what it's like to possess every material object imaginable. Nor do I feel the need to. A good pizza on a Friday is special. Seeing beauty in a million little things is special.

I'm putting my pen down, getting up from my chair, and heading to the kitchen. Be warned, world: I'm going to touch something. I like the kitchen—sometimes even more than my bedroom. It depends on my mood. I open the refrigerator. Nothing's broken here. Beer or soft drink? I didn't even look at the liquor cabinet. I'm showing self-discipline. It's noon, so I'll just take a soft drink. Close the door. The light goes out—at least, I think so. This proves that I don't break everything.

Nuts & Bolts: "Touching" is an important word. Touching goes a long way in making someone feel genuinely cared for. A hand on the shoulder is fine, and a hug is even better to show how you feel. Experiencing this with one companion for four decades has been joyful, and the rewards have been incredible. If you have a companion, try doing the dance together. You might step on a few toes, but no one is watching anyway. If you don't have a dance partner, hang in there. I believe there is someone for each of us.

Story 5
Traveling and Other Marital Advice

I remember a trip I took with a friend. It was a hunting trip. We called it a business trip, but our wives could see right through it. As I recall, we flew into Omaha. Our hunt was just okay, but the camaraderie was excellent, which is truly the point of a hunt. At the end of the trip, we headed back to the Omaha airport, which was no bigger than a strip mall retail center. We got our tickets and thought we had time for a leisurely lunch—until we didn't. We heard our names called over the intercom. They could have just shouted our names in that little airport. I said, "Lookie here, we must be getting moved up to first class." They weren't upgrading us, but they did wonder why we hadn't gotten on the plane. We hadn't considered the time change. So, I thought I could convince the nice ticket lady to reopen the door and let us swagger on in. She said the FAA didn't allow passengers on planes once the door is closed. I didn't know that. I also learned that the Omaha flight options were pretty limited. The next flight wasn't until the following day.

My first thought was that there was no need to keep staff around for the afternoon because no planes were scheduled to depart. My CEO brain never quite shuts down. I thought this, but didn't say it. These were really nice people.

Well, my traveling companions were in a panic. They weren't nearly as experienced in inept traveling as I was. In particular, my colleague, Rob, seemed a bit desperate. He contemplated scaling the fence to chase down the plane, and he also thought about renting a car and driving 20 hours home. A creative idea—but not a good one. He reminded me that he had a two-week-old newborn at home. I didn't mention that it was a fine time to bring up his lack of parenting consideration. I told him he had years to address his short-sightedness, but this didn't alter his thoughts.

Women possess an extra sense that men lack, and they keep it quite secret. They can tell when something is off. I had already cushioned the impact by asking my travel team if they had ever seen the movie "Ferris Bueller's Day Off." They all nodded in agreement. I explained that we were going to do precisely what Ferris would do with a full day to fill, but without a parade, of course. Then, I went back to get the rental car.

Then trouble struck. My comrade, Rob, had a call coming in. We all looked at his phone. I quickly ordered, "Don't answer it." Usually, he was pretty obedient, but not this time. "Hello. We missed our plane." The phone began to bounce off the side of his head. Rob had to switch ears just to let the scolding, crying mother of his child finish her rant. In a weeping voice, she expressed how disappointed she was. Note to all wives: always tell your spouse you are disappointed if you want to make an impact. Calling us a dumbass isn't very effective; we already know that. "Disappointed" is hard to refute. It works on kids, too.

You see, my reason for calling a time-out was to shape our story. I was already working on our tale. It started with a proactive call saying, "Honey, we're okay," and we would fill in the blanks from there. Why? As an on-the-spot marriage counselor, our somewhat exaggerated story would prevent both parties from suffering the severe consequences of our ineptness. His wife would take great comfort in knowing her husband was OK. How you tell the story helps keep priorities in order. Yes, it was a mistake, but fundamentally, all was well. Some might call it lying. I call it shaping drama to avoid trauma.

Anyway, disappointment was waiting at home. What choice do we have? Let's enjoy our day. We started at a Cabela's store. I wandered through the hunting department. I caught my friend looking for things with pink on them. I told him this wasn't the place to buy makeup gifts. Nor would Victoria's Secret. He kept his wallet in his pocket. A material purchase would suggest that someone's love could be bought.

After that, we headed into a Barnes & Noble bookstore. OK, this is not what Ferris would do, but it was raining outside. Plus, I'm four times as old as he was when he made the movie. This is an old person's version of a rainy day. And here we are in Omaha. No offense intended.

Then we went to the movies. My travel companions are beginning to loosen up. Amazing what an oversized Coke and all-you-can-eat popcorn can do. We finished the outing with margaritas and fajitas. Even talked about what we would do if we had another day. We didn't drink too many margaritas, but we did have a great time. It was 10 o'clock, and we made excellent use of the day. We boarded the plane the next morning and were home by 11 am. I never asked how Rob's homecoming went. They are still happily married, so some questions just don't need to be asked.

Got to thinking. I had provided some great marital advice to my young male staff. I decided to write some of it down. Of course, most of my suggestions have never been recorded in any marital counselor how-to books. I don't plan on going into the marital counseling business. I have a hard enough time keeping my marriage intact—I meant to say vibrant.

Here's my advice: when your wife says let's not buy anything for each other this Christmas, do it anyway. It's a slight test of the marital waters, one in which you will fail if you don't have some surprises in your underwear drawer. Not some fancy bedroom outfit. I am talking about diamond earrings. So, be prepared when she brings out an item you've been obsessed with. Stock up on cards, too. I hate it when you realize it's your anniversary and come home from work to a cold shoulder. Consider a gift card or two for massages and pedicures. I don't recall my students writing down my advice, but I bet they have presents stashed away. There is nothing worse than getting caught with your pants down—unless you intended to have your pants down.

I've got all kinds of marital advice. I'm going to save some for my syndicated TV show. But I hope everyone on Earth can find companionship. I know some won't, and it bothers me. Nothing is more fulfilling than a full-time commitment to someone who knows me pretty well, for better or worse. And there have been plenty of worse. I just encourage all to work it out. Why? Some will say they like half their stuff too much. For me, life has felt complete by having my companion at my side for over four decades.

Nuts & Bolts: The most valuable life experience a person can have is a relationship with another. No possession ever compares, nor does reviewing financial statements and admiring the zeros to the left of the decimal point. Pursue companionship, whether as a significant other or a friend. Life improves through stories with your partner. Be sure to document your own.

CHAPTER 5

Pull The Trigger

Hunting Stories

Story 1
Ducks Win

This story is about duck hunting—my many failed attempts. It's more about the ducks winning. "Duck" can refer to several storylines. A punch is thrown—better duck! I could have used this advice a few times. Swimming like a duck means you're thrashing furiously under the water, while on top, you appear as cool as a cucumber. I don't fully understand what it means to be as cool as a cucumber. I often say things without knowing what they mean.

But when it comes to ducks, I have some serious stories. I'm sure a lot of people root for the ducks. I'm okay with the ducks winning sometimes. When they lose, it's mortal—no chance for a replay. The stakes are pretty high. When the hunter loses, he doesn't get his picture taken after the hunt—pretty low stakes. I do feel guilty sometimes. What compels me to do it anyway? The camaraderie, the stories, the immediate thrill of success that so frequently eludes us. This isn't something new; our ancestors saw it as crucial to their survival. People might judge me for this, but it's who I am. To those who aren't hunters, I can empathize with the feeling that this is an unnecessary event. I would like to point out that all creatures we consume are victims of the same experience I had while duck hunting.

The cooked ducks are usually enjoyed at the dinner table, which justifies the activity. Most ducks are plant eaters, and those tend to be the tastiest. However, there are fish-eating ducks, such as mergansers, which are considered inedible due to their strong, gamey flavor and are often shot accidentally or on particularly slow days. I've never eaten one, but I understand they are pretty nasty. Coots, another water-dwelling duck that's a bottom feeder, are generally looked upon as not a dinner table delicacy as well. You would only shoot one accidentally. The cormorant, an invasive bird species in South Carolina, negatively impacts the ecology by consuming fish that amount to three times their weight in a day. They're quite reviled. The Department of Natural Resources provides guidelines for proper disposal once they are killed, and I don't think they refer to it as a funeral. These birds need to be removed to prevent our fish population from being decimated. Therefore, hunters play a positive role in controlling the population of this invasive species.

My Dad was a hunter, so at an early age, we would put on insulated underwear and head out to an island on Lake Wateree. It was an unremarkable lake in the heart of South Carolina that offered Rochesters plenty of recreation as we grew up ten miles away. Fishing, waterskiing, hunting—we made great use of this body of water. We went frequently. It felt like every Saturday. We would bring hot chocolate and lots of snacks. I loved chocolate doughnuts and acted like there was nutritional value in those brown pastries by eating many of them. I loved going with my Dad when I was around six or seven years old. Somehow, he made even boredom fun. We were on this little island, which would have made others want to leave after a short time due to the lack of duck activity. My Dad would tell jokes; sometimes he'd bring a friend along, and I'd listen to their stories. I felt proud of my Dad when he was the hero in one of his tales. I can't recall us harvesting a duck on that island, but I do remember a whole flock flying in to our decoys one day while we stood around a fire he had helped me build. We never got a shot at a single duck, but we talked about it all season. The ducks won that day.

As I grew older, we pursued our passion for early morning trips in semi-cold weather. We went to the coast near Edisto Island. It's considered a Bohemian beachfront where a pair of cutoffs and a t-shirt is all that was necessary for our summer vacation. It was a semi-popular destination for budget vacations. Dad was pretty frugal. We got up at 2:00 am and drove for three hours. We hunted and then drove home. We didn't support the hospitality industry. My Mom even packed lunch for us, which meant there would be no more chocolate donuts. By this time, I had a younger brother who was a way better shot than I was. I liked to pull the trigger first. Dad said I was firing a warning shot, but I didn't think that was funny.

Typically, we had a 2-3 bird morning—a long way to travel to have such a small stringer of feathered carcasses. When I was 13 years old, on a brisk January day, when all conditions were perfect, pandemonium broke out. It felt like we were invisible, with ducks coming in from every direction. Hundreds of ducks. To those readers who are nature lovers, stop reading... because we annihilated them. It was a rare and exceptional day, marked by an 18-bird morning. We immortalized the great bird attack story for the rest of our storytelling days, even when Dad was no longer around to embellish how it all happened. I was a horrible shot; I shot where they were rather than where they were going. It was a day we hoped to experience and had only read about in Field & Stream. One hunting dream was realized. Hunting is about stories, and it's only valuable because you have someone to share it with.

Dad was also a source of entertainment. Once, he went out to retrieve a bird. My brother and I argued over who shot it. Anyone from the Low country of South Carolina knows what pluff mud is like. It is akin to quicksand, only worse. The more you struggle, the more it pulls you into its dark, brown, smelly abyss. The heavier you are, the faster it drags you down. My brother and I paused our argument long enough to be amused by our Dad's toiling as he battled the pluff mud. I don't know why we got so much satisfaction watching our Dad struggle, but we were definitely laughing. Finally, after his waders sank up to his crotch, he declared the effort fruitless. He called in reinforcements: my brother and me. He would have preferred some empathetic adult, but he got us instead. He instructed us to get into our little Jon boat and hoist him out. Being an obedient yet typical 12-year-old, I fumbled while getting the boat into the water. My 10-year-old brother helped, too. We felt like two pirates on a ship. We paddled out to the distressed duck hunter, which was a good 25 yards away. After a lengthy discussion, we decided to pull up beside him. We organized ourselves so he could brace himself on the boat, and all three of us heaved to get him out. It worked. Well, sort of. We got Dad out, but not his waders. They were deeply embedded in the mud that seemed to consume everything. We spent the rest of the morning fishing out Dad's waders. Heaven forbid we leave these $20 rubber, leaky, waterproof materials in the mud. I don't believe my Dad was ecologically motivated; he wanted to show his sons how to be frugal. He was good at that. And entertaining.

I remember one trip to the Outer Banks of North Carolina—a seven-hour drive to Cedar Island. From there, you take a car ferry to Ocracoke Island. American history at its finest. Many who call it home are descendants of Blackbeard's pirates. Only 500 people live there. It's bohemian and rustic. People don't care what you wear, whether it's flip-flops or shorts. It's counter-culture, home to all the nudist colonies and AA meetings since drinking is not allowed. There are 13 miles of beaches, all part of the National Park, with no homes. We had two stake blinds off the backside of Ocracoke Island, an 18-foot Jon boat ride away. A stake blind is an eight-by-eight wooden box elevated six to eight feet above the water and four feet tall. You climb inside, crouch down, and sit. You spend your morning gazing at the horizon of nothing but water. You'd think ducks would have communicated the risk of flying around these obvious manmade boxes. We sat in the boxes and waited for the opportunity to take the shot. We just built the blind—it's a code of honor. Everyone understands that the blind belongs to the builder.

Many ducks have learned the risks of flying recklessly around our wooden box. They understand that they are in danger. A Bluebird Day is when the sun is shining, and there's no wind. The three layers of clothing you chose to protect against the elements come off because it's so warm. This day typically features the ducks winning again. Ducks are more active when it's cold and windy. Most people prefer to sit by the fire on a chilly day, but cold days are actually the best for duck hunting. The worst situation when duck hunting is a day when nature calls. We won't get into the details, but you find yourself in the blind on one of those slow days, unable to stop thinking about your pressing need for a #2 experience. #1 can be awkward, but at least that can be managed.

Dad finally decided he had to give in. This meant he was abandoning our eight-by-eight jail cell to attend to more important business. My brother and I were bored out of our minds. We had already eaten our lunch by 8:30 am, told every hunting story we could think of, and bragged about every self-promoting activity in our lives. We were looking out the blind, examining the sky, when we heard a splash. As Dad prepared to shove off (he liked to use nautical terms), he lost his footing while exiting the blind. Dad was no longer in the boat but in the water, doing this backstroke thing.

We couldn't stop laughing as he moved his arms and legs like a snow angel. He goes to great lengths to prevent anything bad from ever happening, so we loved it when something like this occurred. I never asked him how this calamity impacted his need to use the bathroom; I was too busy laughing until my belly ached. He didn't find the humor in this situation. Once we pulled him out of the water, he did chuckle a bit. He told us to let this be a lesson for us boys. He said that a lot, especially after we witnessed incidents like his decision to take a dip in the middle of winter, fully clothed. He decided it was time to pack up and directed us to pick up the decoys. He was good at bossing us around, too. I also became quite skilled at it. My brother and I were ready to go home—it was time for a nap—The End.

Nuts & Bolts: One of my greatest joys in life is remembering these adventures with my Dad and brother. I hope it inspires you to create your own.

Story 2
Didn't See That Coming

I love pranks, but some rules of engagement are necessary. Pranks should be directed at a known audience. It's unfair to trick some hapless person who can't retaliate. I believe it's wrong to watch TV shows where someone is placed in an ethical dilemma without time to think. Left to our human instincts, the fight-or-flight response can embarrass an unsuspecting person. Additionally, the prankster must realize that karma can be a harsh reality. One should anticipate an equally challenging circumstance for the victim, sort of an eye for an eye. I would prefer a tooth for a tooth. And there's no statute of limitations; I've been reminded of that before.

Okay, so I could be the commissioner of pranks. It should be a high-paying job with two clear guidelines for pranksters. There is to be no lasting harm. And, you must expect consequences. If you can't abide by these two rules of engagement, stick to checkers for entertainment.

My favorite pranks happen within the family, and my Dad loved the art of pulling someone's leg. I don't know why it's called pulling someone's leg, a phrase that dates back to the Neanderthal days, I believe. Maybe back then, they actually pulled someone's leg off. That sounds painful. I think playing tricks is part of my family's DNA. If that's the case, I can blame my passion for pranks on genetics. I wish I had inherited a slightly higher IQ instead. Some better looks would have been nice, or being born into a wealthier family. I suppose I'll stick with my flawed family tree. It has produced a lot of laughs over the years. Turns out, there's nothing better than belly-aching laughter.

I've always enjoyed teasing my younger brother. Being bigger and a bit more experienced than your trusting younger brother means you're less likely to face the same consequences. It feels somewhat like exploiting an inferior species, or maybe it's the survival of the fittest.

One of my favorite games was "Let's see what happens when...". So, I stuck my brother with a cattle prod. But that wasn't really a prank; I did it out of boredom. He didn't take it well. It was no laughing matter and nearly brought the parental judicial system into play. I couldn't let that happen, so I agreed to do his chores for a month. He would have preferred to stick me with the cattle prod to even the score. I imagined him doing it in the middle of the night. I value my sleep too much to risk that.

The best prank I pulled on him happened years later during a long, fruitless hunting trip. My brother Dan, my friend Bill, and I were out duck hunting. We hadn't pulled the trigger all day. I can hear the cheers from the non-hunting readers. Dan dozed off, and I thought it might be funny to remove the shells from his gun. So, I did. The stars aligned, and after a long half-day of waiting, a flock of geese flew straight to our blind. We had the perfect setup. We threw up our guns. Bill and I fired away with great success.

Meanwhile, my brother squeezed his trigger several times but managed to get no shots from his gun. After we retrieved our haul, Bill asked me when I would tell Dan what I had done. I told him never. And I never did, until years later, when I shared the story with friends over a beer. Dan tried to figure out how he had made such a foolish mistake. We had a great laugh at his expense, and in the end, he joined in the laughter.

He one-upped me, though. Of course, he would, since we share the same prankster DNA. The scene was set when I decided that my new hobby would be beer brewing. My partner in this endeavor was Larry, the gynecologist. It's not necessarily a profession that guarantees high-quality beer, but I assumed he had done a few chemistry experiments along the way. My qualifications were terrible. I dislike following written directions, especially when they are unclear. Plus, I had never completed a chemistry experiment. I'm not sure why I thought brewing beer would be fun, other than I enjoy drinking it. Long story short, I spent a couple of thousand dollars on equipment and ingredients. I wasted a lot of time, stunk up my wife's kitchen, and never managed to make a decent six-pack.

I decided to become a beer critic instead. One family vacation, my brother piped up and said he was brewing beer. I tried to forewarn him that our gene pool would not allow success, but he said it was too late. I said, "Let's see what you got."

He quickly removes a brown bottle from the refrigerator, pops the cap, and hands it to me, the beer expert. I examine it for cloudiness and sediment, just like any critic should. I raised it to my lips, still maintaining my frown, and cast a slight look of disgust. I considered what my poor brother would need to do to make this liquid palatable. Unable to restrain myself, I began lecturing him on his brave yet insufficient efforts. Unfortunately, there were accomplices in the testing lab, and by this time, tears streamed down their faces. My brother did a good job pretending to hang on to every critical word I uttered.

When I paused to inhale, he revealed that this was not his creation but a recipe that had been around for 400 years. He had soaked the label off a Bass Ale. Um, the room could hardly contain itself. Did I mention that I believe in karma? Everyone, myself included, had a good belly-aching laugh about that.

Nuts & Bolts: By creating funny situations, life becomes more interesting. And the world is a better place when life is interesting. Do leave the cattle prod to the cows.

Story 3
Another Duck Story

Our duck hunting trips were usually a reasonable drive from home. Once I reached working age, I could afford to pay for a flight and travel to places with substantial duck populations. With this financial shift, something else also changed. The role of the hunt director began to evolve.

We visited Lake Catherine in central Canada, located just across the border from Detroit, several times over a decade. Our trips didn't involve five-star accommodations; we weren't looking to be pampered. Particular in this area, the duck guides are not known for organizing or maintaining their equipment. My brother and I relied on divine intervention to make circumstances work. Dad didn't subscribe to this plan. He carried the infamous canary yellow pad with all the supplies he could think of, checked off. One item that was immediately checked off was the sense of adventure—gone.

I remember our first day on our Canadian hunting trip in 1993. We arrived at the boat landing only to find an Evin rude 20-horse motor broken down into pieces. The guide said it was fine, which was good enough for me. Why not trust a new acquaintance whose appearance suggested they might not have completed school, and the tattoos were of the nature that one finds from doing time? If that were true, most likely, he couldn't legally handle a weapon, but I decided not to ask too many questions. Dad thought it was necessary to give the motor a thorough inspection to minimize the risk of putting us in danger with our new, though not completely trusted, friend. The sun was rising as Dad began to work on the mess. He seemed to know what he was doing, but the sun was growing fast, and anyone who knows anything about duck hunting understands that time is of the essence.

Dad wouldn't hear any of it. He spent an hour correcting everything the guide had overlooked throughout the season. All the guides had nicknames; ours was Wolff- we didn't ask why. After Dad fixed the motor while his two unhelpful adult kids looked on, we were finally on our way. Dad was right— the ducks flew all morning. The time we took didn't impact our efforts, and we had a good reason to get a picture taken by the end of the hunt.

Wolff ended up being our favorite guide; he really took care of my Dad. If my guess that he served time was accurate, it truly helped him master the art of customer service. The only thing we didn't like was his tendency to drive 90 miles an hour in a late-model, uninspected car. We weren't in a hurry. We learned not to tip until we were going home at the end of the trip. Duck guides seem to need to celebrate excessively once rewarded for their efforts. If we tip too soon, the next day may not start until noon—or maybe never. I remember going to a guide's house because he hadn't shown up, only to discover he had a woman with him. I assumed she wasn't his wife, but that was none of my business, so I didn't ask. He didn't get mad; he needed tip money to repeat the previous night. I appreciate someone who is a motivated customer service provider. He got dressed, and off we went. We had a great day of hunting. We paid him just before we left to return home. It was another excellent day.

By 2003, in a remote Canadian town, the hunt director's role changed during one of our ragamuffin trips. We flew to Detroit, as usual, picked up the rental van, and drove to a First Nations reservation on Lake Catherine. Upon arrival, this minivan we had rented had mechanical issues that created a noise under the hood, which was very concerning. My brother and I weren't as concerned as Dad, who always had the infamous canary yellow pad. He wanted us to take a day off, get the car repaired, and hunt the next day.

I was starting to feel my oats. I was now the self-appointed captain of our family hunting team, responsible for the success of the trips to chase feathered waterfowl. Yes, our rental van was running on two cylinders and looked like one of those cars you see in crime TV shows. The ruckus under the hood had us all a bit worried about where it might stop. However, our goal was to make it to the boat landing 20 miles away. That's all I cared about. Dad asked, "What if it breaks down on the return trip, after we are done hunting?" He was concerned. "How would you figure getting back to the hotel and then to the airport?"

Dad planted his flag and declared we were not hunting. We would spend the day waiting for someone to repair our broken-down but running vehicle, which clearly only used two of its six cylinders. I had a different declaration: we were going hunting. It was a standoff. My brother stayed out of the argument—something he often chose to do.

My father laid out his case. We were in a foreign country with a vehicle that was clearly at risk of breaking down. In essence, we could be shipwrecked on land. He was right. Still, I argued that we only had three days to hunt. I couldn't care less about this piece of junk van. We would take our chances. My Dad made the obvious point of asking what we would do if our transportation failed us.

It only took me a second to spit out the plan. Earlier in the day, I had noticed a Chevrolet dealership across the street from our motel, which was fifty years old and included breakfast. I said, "Well, if the van breaks down, we'll park wherever it stops. Get a taxi to the motel. Then I'll visit the dealership and I will buy a car to drive us all the way home." And I meant it. Even if it meant explaining to my wife upon my return why this trip resulted in us owning a new car. Defeated, he conceded.

Out we went with our same guide, Wolff, our designated driver, going 90 miles an hour, hanging on for dear life. We made it, and no new car purchase was necessary. More importantly, I thought at the time that I wore my captain hat well that trip.

In retrospect, it was an awkward moment. Dad felt challenged, and I wanted him to feel challenged. If I had it to do all over again, I would make my Dad feel more important. He felt discouraged because I didn't value his advice. Later in life, my response to him would have been, "Dad, you taught me to be an independent thinker. So I probably don't give your advice as much credence as I could. You taught me to solve my problems in my own way." As a Dad myself these days, I wish my thoughts were more welcomed by my children.

But at the time, there were still moments when Dad enjoyed me being the responsible party. He got to laugh while I handled everything. By then, I was paying for his trips, and he just crossed his arms to watch me face the adventures of traveling. On one long journey home, he found humor in an airline steward who had taken an interest in me. The handsome steward laid down two empty mini bottles of vodka on my tray and asked if I was Steve Young because I looked a lot like him. I do, truth be told, but I didn't want this guy drawing attention to it. Dad asked who Steve was, and I told him he was a football quarterback. Dad was getting a kick out of watching the steward try to score a date. I'm delighted with my wonderful wife and three kids—no offense to the steward. Dad called me Steve Young for a while, followed by laughter.

I remember one of the last times when Dad retook charge on a hunt. To provide context, you must understand that duck guides are fascinating creatures. We aren't prudes, but we don't like guides telling jokes about women's body parts or discussing sexual acts in the company of our family. We're just weird about this topic, I guess. The guide was on his fourth or fifth story about some sexual act he either imagined or claimed to have experienced. I would think he would have checked out the audience before going into this monologue. Dad spoke up once the guide paused long enough to catch his breath and said, "I tell you what, if I give you $100, can my boys and me hunt by ourselves?" The flustered but money-driven guide responded with something like, "You got a deal," and he left the blind. That was when $100 was a pretty big tip for a hunting guide. I had never seen my Dad pull out a $100 bill before. It didn't affect my inheritance, but I knew he meant business. Everyone went home happy. The guide may have had another group that enjoyed hearing his stories.

That year, I stopped hunting with my Dad. It's not that we grew bored with our hobby; he simply got older and passed away.

Nuts & Bolts: Don't put off what you can do today until tomorrow. I'm getting old, too. My only regret is that I wish I had more duck stories to share with my Dad.

Story 4
The Last Duck Hunting Story– I Promise

There's something about marking the calendar for the Saturday before Thanksgiving. Memories rush through my mind, typically exaggerated versions of my hunting trips with my Dad and brother, pulling out all the camouflage gear and recalling the glory days, the massive success of our shoots – all stories that verge on pure vanity, but in a harmless way.

Vanity hurts when it hits our pocketbooks. The most vain members of our society are hunters. We must own the latest fashion trends in camouflage. The pricier, the better. This means the animals we hunt can be misled more easily by the latest designs that attempt to mimic Mother Nature. Ducks are more likely to be tricked by my Desert Storm patterns than by old-school styles. Clearly, ducks are becoming trendier over time.

Sidebar: Golf equipment provokes vanity. Every year, they make new models that far exceed the performance of your old relics. It fits under the red candy theory. We always want what someone else possesses. For non-golfers, participants always admire the shiny new clubs of their peers. A well-known reality is that clubs have little impact on your score. It is more dependent on your ability and knowledge of the game. Investing in lessons is a better use of our dollars than the newest technology. But we golfers just can't say no. "Ten more yards," you say. Go ahead and ring it up. Funny, the game would be obsolete if every advertisement for more distance with a golf club were valid. Those who say golf clubs are their favorite possessions see them only in a temporary state. Next year's models are on the way. Pure vanity.

If I'm going to be honest about my vanity, it was my excessive pride in my dog, Maddie. I didn't even face my wife's disapproval with this canine acquisition; she just bought another horse. We both kept our mouths shut and enjoyed a happy marriage. Enough about marriage. Maddie and I started hunting with some new friends in some really nice places. She was a yellow lab, initially thought to be a waste of money. My Dad's friend, a talented dog trainer, saw nothing redeemable in Maddie. He told me, "I'm glad I didn't tell you to buy that dog." It took some time, and we proved him wrong. Maddie blossomed and became a retrieving machine.

Maddie was the pride of my existence. If I walked in the room, her eyes would immediately turn to me and greet me with a tail wagging that asked, What can I do for you now? She followed up with other questions like, Well, are you ready to go take a walk? When will you throw some dummies to practice preparing for our upcoming hunting opportunities? All she wanted to do was bring me happiness. Maddie became my pleasant distraction, which I enjoyed when I came home from a rough day at work. The kids had grown up and moved on with their families. I was still proud of my wife; however, she often questions my motives for acting happy to see her. Many times, she was right; I had an ulterior motive. Now, I'm returning to my dog story. Whether doves or ducks, Maddie performed without complaint when I failed to see any birds fall. She found every fowl and became my reliable copilot.

I became part of a duck club. Maddie, who recently passed away, was my best hunting companion, and I want you to know her. This story features Maddie at her best.

A common occurrence the night before the hunt is sitting around the fire, drinking something brown to loosen the tongue. The goal is to outdo the storyteller who spoke before you. This could go late into the evening and be risky; the late hours and drinking might impair your shooting ability. However, it doesn't affect the dogs' performance. Many hunters share tales about great hunts from the past, some of which are truthful, while others are just boasting. They often brag about their shooting skills and the exceptional qualities of their dogs. I try to stay quiet when discussing my shooting or my dog, Maddie.

I remember one night sitting around the fire when a guy talked about the exceptional abilities of his Special Lab. I'll admit I felt a little intimidated. Maddie was in her kennel, sleeping soundly. She was perfectly capable of navigating a string of decoys to reach a wounded duck trying to escape, but she couldn't walk on water. The Lab described that night around the fire sounded like it had extraordinary skills. I started to doubt whether Maddie would be able to keep up. I went to bed thinking, should I leave my dog in the kennel because I didn't want to embarrass her and my colleagues if she struggled to perform. The thought crossed my mind that I should throw in the white flag now.

The next day, it was show time—a cup of coffee was mandatory. A group of uneasy hunters waited for the safety speech. We made our way to the blinds with a guide. It seems a bit chaotic, but pampered folks in a duck club can prepare for their hunt much easier than regular hunters who freelance. The former has a guide to handle the work. It's not as dramatic, but it's probably not as fun as freelancing, either.

Morning light. Guns go off. It always starts a few minutes before legal shooting time, because hunters just can't help themselves. You see birds fall. Corn, millet, and chufa float around to entice hungry birds to risk it all for this tasty meal. Maddie has made several successful retrieves with my guests close by and observing. I feel as proud of her as I do of my son when he hit a double in a Little League baseball game. So far, it's been an ideal morning, and I'm happy as can be. My concerns about Maddie have abated, and I'm enjoying her precise skills.

Out of the blue, our guide looks over to tell us to watch the Special Lab. I turn my attention and wonder if Maddie will be outdone. This dog acted like a stray from the pound. He was going every which way except toward the fowl. At the top of his lungs, after forcing his dog into the water, Mr. Fire Circle Braggard shouted, "Damnit!!!" Hence, the guides all nicknamed the lab "Damnit." It was clear the dog wasn't meeting his expectations. It didn't meet ours either. At first, we couldn't help but laugh as Mr. Braggard threw rocks at the dead duck, trying to guide his dog into a proper retrieval. However, the situation quickly shifted from entertaining to annoying. Even hungry wild birds could sense that something was off. That morning, the owner of Special Lab realized that his Lab was not quite as Special as he had advertised.

Once the hunt was over, the guide from the blind with Damnit approached and asked to borrow Maddie. I can't help but smile about it even now, years later. Being a staple of the South, I forced myself to be humble. My Cinderella became the Princess in the ballroom. What a proud moment. This dog that others have dismissed as completely useless became the hero of the day. I genuinely believe that it was the weeks and months of love that I poured into Maddie that transformed her into a success. It didn't matter that my shooting was questionable. Maddie was the belle of the ball.

I told Damnit's owner that Maddie had faced tough days as well. I reassured him that I was confident Damnit was a good dog. There would be great activities to share with Damnit: a couch on Saturday afternoon, watching football, maybe barking at the UPS guy when he came by, or chewing up all the furniture. At the next hunt, there was no mention of Damnit around the campfire. No need to brag about Maddie, either.

Nuts & Bolts: It's okay to be vain about a dog who overcame many obstacles to become the best hunting dog ever. What I learned from Maddie is that if human beings showed the same appreciation for each other that their pets do to them, the world would be a much more desirable place to be.

And stop wasting money on all the camouflage gear!

Story 5
Shooting The Bird

It might seem like a paradox, but I evolved into being an ardent environmentalist through my love of hunting. Mother Nature plays a crucial role in creating ideal hunting conditions. Good weather is essential. Rain is a vital requirement for establishing optimal breeding conditions and producing crops that animals can feed on.

Sidebar: Ironically, farmers are devoting less time to tilling the soil and growing crops. Being dedicated to farming doesn't yield enough reward. It's really a shame that small farmers have to seek work elsewhere. However, for good hunting results, Mother Nature needs to be your ally.

To hunt well, you need to understand the weather, the ways of animals, and the quality of the soil. My passion for hunting and the incredible memories it has given me connect me to the earth. One example is the search to find the best spot for hunting; you must be attuned to your surroundings. I recall the first time I achieved success in this area. It was the opening day of dove season, and my son was 9 years old. Here in South Carolina, the opening day of dove season feels like Christmas in September for those who own camouflage. I recall that there were around 25,000 hunters on the opening day back in the 1970s.

Nowadays, there are far fewer hunters and birds than there were in the past. Still, many neighbors eagerly anticipate the Saturday before Labor Day. Most hunts kick off with a barbecue and sweet tea. Alcohol was frowned upon until after the spectacle. The quest to snag the best spot, which means having all the birds flying low nearby, starts immediately. One lucky day, I hit the jackpot and secured the best place. I harvested five birds before anyone else even got a shot off, and there were 30 people in the field. I was shooting well, with my 9-year-old son acting as my retriever. I didn't put a collar on him, and no whistle was needed either; he was right on target. I finished shooting my limit in just 20 minutes. Everyone was happy to see me leave the field, but no applause came my way.

My love of hunting has been misunderstood over the years. A few years ago, I remember working with a young woman from Canada. I'll call her Donna. One of my vendor partners had asked me to help train one of their new employees. Donna was sent down to learn how to sell construction materials. We were calling on architects and successfully promoting her company. We had many conversations and got along well.

In a curious and friendly way, she asked me what I was doing on Saturday. I recall the stoplight in Charlotte, NC, where we waited for the light to turn green. I told her I was dove hunting. She had never heard of it. She asked why I spent my precious time on earth hunting little birds. I let my guard down and told her how euphoric it felt when you pulled the trigger, and this target folded up on its way to the ground. Our friendly relationship immediately took an abrupt turn. She made sure the car door was unlocked. I didn't want to apologize for my interest in hunting as a hobby. This practice dates back to the earliest stages of human existence. Responsible hunting helps maintain ecological balance and provides sustenance for human beings to survive. However, I should have told Donna that I was working in a soup kitchen all day Saturday.

Back to my story on responsible dove hunting. This activity typically involves a group, with participants positioned 50 to 60 yards apart. If you're successfully shooting, everyone knows. If you miss the target, everyone knows. There's pressure to perform, and if you miss frequently, it can lead to performance anxiety. I've heard about this in the bedroom and witnessed it on the dove field.

We all go through phases, ranging from making every shot to not knowing how to hit those feathered torpedoes. Often, when someone else is shooting, I'm rooting for the birds. When they miss, I pretend I didn't see it. The goal is to hit the legal limit, and sometimes that happens. As I did yesterday, I shot well but lacked a big enough audience. It would have been nice to have more hunters around to share my accolades.

I clean and eat all the birds I retrieve. That's most of them, even though they can be hard to spot once they stop flying. It can be perplexing when you walk to the exact spot where the bird fell, only to be shocked to find nothing. You end up walking around in circles of disbelief. If the bird isn't found, you return to your stool and replay the incident in your mind–how could this have happened? It's one of the more minor mysteries that perplexes me, while the bigger mystery of the complex beauty of Nature always intrigues me.

Nuts & Bolts: While we inhabit this revolving blue marble, we must take care of what we have here and not neglect the beautiful gifts that surround us. Take someone along to enjoy the day with you. Define the day not by the success at the end of a barrel but by being amidst creation with others. Reflect on the fantastic experience of exploring our planet. Not just concrete or pavement, but dirt and what grows from it. Mother Nature puts on the most incredible show on earth. Find a way to see it today, with or without a gun in your lap.

CHAPTER 6

Stories Inspired by Golf

&

Other Balls

Story 1
FORE!

For those who don't play golf, I highly recommend using your remaining time on earth for other activities. Why? Golf brings such heartbreak. It exposes your worst characteristics. Church deacons are victims of the temptation to cheat while playing golf. We should hold a prayer vigil after our rounds, asking for forgiveness and mercy. God, forgive me for claiming a bogey after my eighth shot failed to put a ball in a hole.

Shouldn't there be a greater reward for a nice tee shot? It means nothing unless you follow it up with two or three additional miraculous contacts with a golf ball. Why does the ball seem to find the worst destination? It lands in high grass. Or a divot. Maybe behind a tree. It's remarkable how many people have been drawn into playing this game. These are smart people, too! Can't we find a more stimulating way to spend our spare time? Compared to golf, work feels like a hobby. When an admin assistant quits, a big account takes their business elsewhere, or your boss reports how far behind you are on sales goals– all those consequences are better than striking a stick against a dimpled ball. Inadvertently, I might add. Golf feels like punishment when you have never sinned until you shout words you usually wince at when hearing.

It is expensive, too. You must show up wearing a logoed shirt from a PGA event you attended–shocking how a small logo can add immense value to a garment. Last week, on the golf course, one guy in my foursome said he would start a GoFundMe to buy me new golf shoes. They thought it was funny. He got into my head, and I missed the putt. And he's a friend! Or was. We all pledge allegiance to the newest equipment, guaranteeing that 20 yards will be added to the result of our wayward tee shot. I'm of the belief that they share the same marketing firm as those makers of blue pills, promising our companions will love us more. I never tried one of those pills. But I have bought new clubs pretty often. Perhaps I should think more about my wife than golf. On second thought, I believe my wife is OK with me choosing a new putter instead.

We even devised ways to make cheating (at golf!) acceptable by folks who are otherwise morally responsible, saying that the putt is good. We allow this cheating to prevent the owner of the ball from experiencing more failure. It's saving face. I actually like this form of charity, and it pisses me off when my fellow players refuse to extend this gracious overture. I have choked frequently, attempting to hit a perfectly round ball 3 feet in a straight line. Another way we like to cheat in golf is to argue whether the ball is within the leather or not, which means the ball is considered to be an accepted distance from the hole to be considered "good." Then, they pick up the ball and go to the next hole. Why does that matter? Extend me the courtesy of giving me the putt.

I have displayed some of my worst behaviors ever while holding a golf club. A few decades ago, I recall playing with my son, Drew, who was not necessarily a future golf phenomenon at the time. We were playing for a small wager, maybe $10. Upon arriving on the 7th hole, I was getting pretty testy. I had missed six short putts in a row. He had not extended the "it's good" courtesy. I asked again if the fairly close putt was good. He said no. I missed. Then, in a fit of sin, I threw my putter a good fifty yards. It landed 10 yards up in a tree—a pretty good toss, I must say.

But now I had a problem. Fortunately, no one was around other than my son and his uncle to witness this temper tantrum. I turned to my product of love and lust and said, "Look what you made me do." It made me feel better, even though it was a complete lie. But I still had a dilemma. How do you get a putter out of a tree? I don't believe many golfers have faced this issue. I took my 7-iron. I'm pretty good with my 7-iron. I threw it right where the putter was wedged. It got stuck, too. I started to sweat. I never thought about packing a chainsaw on my golf cart. I probably would have lost my club privileges, which would be a blessing in disguise. My anxiety was on the rise.

I did the most logical thing I could think of. I reached over to grab a club from my son's bag. Drew threw himself on top of his clubs like he was saving a human being's life. With his club option eliminated, I continued to work with what I had left in my bag. "Work with what you have." I liked that mantra. It served me well for the next throw of my club was successful, and the clubs rained down, proving there is a Golf God. I calmly collected my clubs, and we went to hole 8. I didn't even think about throwing my putter this time. Pretty proud of my self-restraint. I was over my temper tantrum until I got home and listened to Drew tell the story. I hate stories when I'm the reason everyone is belly-aching with laughter. I don't do these things in real life, only when I'm on the stupid, overly manicured patches of grass. These golf superintendents should be ashamed of themselves for spending so much time making the grass look presentable. Can't they find a real job?

In addition to this display of bad behavior, I had another incident on hole 10. I was riding by myself. My son and his uncle were on another cart. This was a deliberate decision, I am sure. We were smoking cigars because you have to do something to make this game tolerable. I accidentally dropped my cigar in my golf bag. Do you know how flammable those old golf bags are? Being the type of person who would run into a fire if necessary, I took action immediately. I unhooked my golf bag and dumped out all the contents by shaking the bag upside down. I mean, all of my clubs. It was a fire. If I had been thinking clearly, I would have let the whole set burn up and would have found a better pastime, like bird watching. Anyway, I put out the inferno while my golf mates watched and wondered if my club-throwing incident had caused a temporary mental disorder. This just wasn't my day.

Golf should be against the law. It's not as serious as a felony, but perhaps comparable to a reckless driving charge. If I were to run for office, banning golf would be high on the list of my political agenda. Just think how much time I can save those golf addicts. Get them to go take up bowling. Flower arranging. Checkers. Anything other than playing a game with a stick and a small, dimpled ball.

Nuts & Bolts: I appreciate all readers who agree with stopping this useless sport. Why call it a sport? It is a distraction like surfing the internet. Golf is ruining lives. Please reach out to all your friends and loved ones. Plead with them not to fall victim to the words, "I think I am going to take up golf." Their life will be better for it. So will the rest of the world.

Story 2
A Black Eye

I recall playing for an adult church basketball team back in the mid-90s. We were playing against the Catholics one night. They were known to be physical. We Methodists are not passive, but we keep our elbows to ourselves. No one asked us about our basketball skills, however, before joining our Methodist congregation. I'm not familiar with what other denominations do. Maybe they Google the prospect to learn about their history—probably not a bad idea. They don't want habitual sinners or bad athletes joining the flock. I'm just kidding about Churches vetting applicants to a church. They hire someone else to do it. No, really, just kidding.

Sidebar: What I like most is that churches welcome anyone and everyone to enter their doors on Sunday. However, there is hope that a few rainmakers will also wander in. Rainmakers are the individuals who can bridge the gap between what has been financially committed and what falls short of the offering plate. Rainmakers are also valuable when considering the construction of an addition, such as a gym, a popular structure among Methodist congregations. It makes an excellent home for the 5th Sunday potluck lunches after church. If you look at a calendar, you will notice there are four 5th Sundays in a year. I really looked forward to these get-togethers. That is, I did until everyone started bringing prepared food from the local grocery store. I prefer the homemade stuff.

A gym also makes an excellent home for good old-fashioned sports competitions. We Methodists have a mantra: We stick to the middle of the road in the Protestant Christian hierarchy. It is not a highbrow church or one with oil spots in the parking lot—it is just in the middle. The same goes for our basketball team. There were no church league championships, but we were not an easy win. Other teams knew it would be a challenge.

I liked basketball. I was not very good at basketball, but I hustled. Eventually, you have to put the slightly undersized ball through a barely larger hoop. It's a funny game. And it taught me some humility.

On this particular night, playing the Catholics, one of my teammates was mouthy. This means he said things that church folks shouldn't. The game got a little heated, and I still couldn't throw the ball through the hoop. I was better at defending, and I like being called a defender; it makes me feel tougher. One of the Catholic guys took a shot. I did my best to hold my position for a rebound. Evidently, my opponent wanted the orange ball more than I did. His elbow caught me in the eye. It must have been pretty hard because it knocked me out. Apparently, the benches cleared. It wasn't very Christian, I guess. But the elbow hit me in such a way that blood was gushing out everywhere, so much so that it stopped the disagreement, I heard later. I never thought that my bloodshed would lead to better Christian behavior. Kind of ecumenical.

I don't remember much, but I heard there was a doctor in the house. I arrived home with somebody who gave me a towel and a big bag of ice. I hope I didn't mess up his car. My wife declared my Christian basketball career was over. I was already ready to give up playing, for I had noticed my pulled muscles, which had been caused by sprinting up and down the court, took a lot longer to heal. I simply wasn't as young as I thought I was.

That night, I insisted on doing what any clear-thinking adult would do: I went to a doctor's friend's home to see if she thought I should go to the hospital. She said not only do I need to go to the hospital, but I may require an overnight stay. She thought I might have a severe concussion. She volunteered to call an ambulance. I left her place as fast as a one-eyed person can muster. Cindy drove me to the emergency room. I am no longer allowed to seek free medical advice before going to the hospital. I'm not sure if Cindy acted like a wife or a mother. Either way, I am following her suggestions. Or orders.

The next day, I could still only see out of one eye. I had a bunch of stitches around the other one. I had to explain some things when I got to the office. I probably gussied up the story to make myself more heroic, but the truth is, I felt chagrin. When you encounter someone with a black eye, your mind always goes to how it happened. You can't help it. People wonder, what did he do? As more people asked, I started to alter my story to evoke some sympathy. No one feels sorry for a church basketball player's black eye. Some folks acted like there was nothing wrong. I always wondered what they were thinking. I got tired of explaining the unfortunate damage to my face. In summary, a black eye is not a fun accessory.

I did have a secretary who greeted me at her desk. She was curious, but not in a bad way. She said she liked the look of a man with a black eye. She said it was sexy. Intriguing. I didn't know what to say. I imagine I mumbled something like, Thank you. She didn't follow me out to my car, and I was happy about that. I guess I wasn't so sexy after all. But she definitely helped me laugh at myself!

Nuts & Bolts: Black eyes are just part of life. Of course, I don't play basketball anymore, but nowadays, I don't even watch it! We all need to put these incidents behind us. Apologize if someone was hurt, but do not let history define you. Set your sights on better days. Make the world better by being different. And keep your elbows to yourself.

Story 3
Just A Funny Story

I told a funny story at dinner last night. It makes me smile to recollect a memory in a humorous way. Give me a choice between learning something interesting or listening to a funny story, and I will end up in the laughing huddle. I can't help it. It probably says something significant about me, but I won't be alone. Knowledge, in this case, is perhaps overrated.

Sidebar: I don't understand how the mind works during dinner conversations. Someone tells a story. Then, someone else tells a story on the same subject in the hopes of one-upping the previous storyteller. After that, maybe another story. It's a version of competitive storytelling. And then, the conversation shifts to a new topic. Hopefully, avoiding politics and sports. If the weather ends up as the subject, it had better be severe. Otherwise, the dinner talk has hit a wall. Then you need to come up with something quickly, such as a funny story you can pull from your arsenal.

Well, here's a story from my arsenal. My industry thrived on pranks, just as my family did. Maybe it was just me, the only common denominator. Warning: Sometimes there's a colleague you don't want to prank. The consequences would be too severe. It is best to stick to those who are not vengeful or very creative.

In my work environment, we frequently have suppliers come to our area. We considered these corporate guys a big distraction—a necessary evil. After wowing them for two or three days, you'd pat them on the back and say, "I really enjoyed your company. See you next year," as you guide them out the door.

Well, my friend, Will, was entertaining a corporate executive, John, who was a sales manager. John was a good sales manager and a good guy. One of the guys you didn't mind showing up. He kept quiet and didn't interrogate. John's timing was crucial to the story. He arrived just days after Will's 50th birthday party.

At these milestone events, it's great to be acknowledged, and Will was recognized with a variety of gag gifts, as we typically do. It's an excellent opportunity for everyone to laugh at your expense. One of his friends felt it was appropriate to gift a rather large facsimile of a man's private part. I didn't know how he mustered up the courage to go in and buy this massive piece of rubber. I'll call it a toy. He probably felt it was necessary to explain to the cashier that it was a gag gift, as if the cashier cared what you did with your new purchase.

I'm sure everyone laughed. I wondered what someone might do intentionally with such a toy. Well, the only thing Will could come up with was to use it to keep the laughs going at someone else's expense. So, Will and John finished their tour around his territory, and it was time for John's departure. Will kindly offered to take John to the airport. In the process of loading the car, the rubber toy was discreetly placed in John's carry-on luggage. All wrapped in aluminum foil.

After exchanging goodbyes at the airport, John does what you do when you go to catch a plane—no need to review the details. While in the TSA line, minding his own business, the TSA inspector reviewing luggage on the conveyor had a frown on his face and determined that John's luggage needed to be inspected. They asked to examine the bag of the confused owner of the suitcase. And he replied, You can look at my stuff, of course.

The silver-wrapped object of interest has surfaced. The TSA agent asked the obvious question: What is this? John answered that he had no clue. Well, the TSA replies, we're going to have to see what's in there. John shrugs and watches curiously. The TSA agent carefully unwrapped the subject of concern. All of a sudden, he jumped back like a rattlesnake had been exposed. Maybe a rattlesnake would have been preferred. The shock of what the package enclosed was being absorbed by all the surrounding parties. I can't help but laugh when I imagine the moment when everyone realized this was not an everyday event.

John was speechless. The TSA crew did not enjoy the humor of the moment. They clearly felt victimized, too. And I'm sure no one wanted to touch it. TSA actually reviewed the list of unacceptable travel items to see if John was in trouble, but this item didn't appear. He was free to travel, albeit embarrassed. He had to travel with the knowledge that he could not inflict retribution for at least a year.

This time, the folks at the dinner party laughed and laughed at this story, and no one could top it. Happily, other funny stories were told, and it was a good night for all.

Nuts & Bolts: These stories need to be told and retold. Why? I'm not sure. But mankind needs to laugh. And it is not all that offensive if you know John. Just enjoy the moment. Scrutinize your luggage when traveling with mischievous friends, especially after milestone birthdays. Enjoy a funny story. And tell me the next one.

Story 4
Watchya Got? I Got Nothing

After a less-than-overachieving round of golf, I'm thinking about what I have. First, I have a card game with friends soon. I also got 65 years of accumulating stuff. Some are material goods—some are memories. And I far prefer the memories. I'm excited to make some memories shortly with my buddies sitting around a card table.

I couldn't make a living playing golf, and I wonder if I could make a living playing cards. On this hot summer night, sitting on a screened-in porch with a fan overhead, trying to convince my fellow players that I have a winning hand is a challenge. I got a lot of convincing to do. My poker face is on full display. However, when I lie, my face reveals everything. I've tried to tell something other than the truth many times, which rarely works. Fortunately, I have some gullible opponents in the game, and I'm making progress. Unfortunately, one guy isn't fooled; he stays in. Why? I don't even think he can name all the suits in a deck. Well, "I've got nothing," I tell the group. And the pot moves away from me.

Oh well. This is a low-stakes game. It's the only type I will play. There's no need to send me to Gamblers Anonymous. I have plenty of issues, but giving away my hard-earned money isn't one of them. I like to say, "I got nothing" in a card game. It makes me feel like I've revealed my flaws before the rest of humanity discovers my shortcomings. I haven't said, "I got nothing," regarding intelligence. I might not have a full deck, but I have enough smarts to use a few multisyllabic words. I sometimes use big words to show off, although mostly out of context. It doesn't matter. Most of my friends have a limited vocabulary.

I got nothing and I got everything. I'm remembering all my accumulated stuff and trying to recall what mattered. Everything is essential when it is new. It's funny how the shine wears off. Maybe the value of a possession could be determined by its timelessness – or how it impacts humanity? It is incredible how hard we work in our lives to have stuff. In the end, we realize that possessions, most of them do not matter. I have yet to see anyone carry them into the afterlife. Of course, I haven't seen the afterlife yet, so I cannot prove my theory that "you can't take it with you."

I do know that possessions are no substitute for a relationship. It amazes me how much stuff can interfere with relationships. Estates come to mind. Fortunately, my brother and I did not let our parents' accumulations get in the way of our feelings for each other. The takeaway to consider is that when a quarrel occurs over a vase, an automobile, or a piece of property, be the first to declare a compromise. Sometimes, this will not work, but attempt to set the tone. Hopefully, an armed conflict or court date can be avoided.

What about reviving the practice of entertaining ourselves with possessions that are free and not made of plastic? I played a lot of army in the woods with nothing more than a stick to defend my fort, and no one suffered injury from my imaginary shooting at the enemy. It was a little challenging to determine a winner of that fantastical war. I guess that could lead to the old saying, "Live to fight another day." I saw the laughter and joy emanating from our ability to make a toy out of something discarded by nature, like a stick. I realize I am old. Playing army is way nostalgic. I have great memories, but I don't recall a favorite stick.

Was I dealt a good hand? We're on to the next game, and I can't tell much about these cards in front of me. There are a lot of unknowns ahead. No one can see the future. Weather forecasters can predict what might happen in a few days. Businesses can see their backlog for the upcoming year. But I can't predict how many days I have ahead of me. I'd better make good use of my time. I think I'm going to call and raise. That's big-shot talk for those who aren't familiar with poker. I enjoy being a big shot, especially when everyone thinks I'm being humble. That doesn't happen very often.

I couldn't predict what would happen after switching to my fourth college major. I started to question if I had a future, and I feared I would end up saying, "I got nothing." The key was to keep looking. Seeking. I enjoy seeking; it feels like I'm trying harder than just looking. You have to search diligently, exploring several opportunities. If you do end up saying, "I got nothing," the response should be to keep seeking. I believe we were put here on this planet to contribute to making the world better each day. Our task is to discover what our mission on earth might be. It can be exciting or overwhelming.

I have been rambling. But with purpose. Don't let possessions define you. Once, a significant hurricane threatened our home. I had to decide what to put in my SUV. Animals came first. Of course, and my wife. (I might have my order wrong.) My wife filled the empty spaces of the car with irreplaceables- probably 20 boxes of photos. She had so much more substance than I did. My only contribution was my favorite shotgun. I guess I am a little shallow. I really like that shotgun. Fortunately, the storm veered out to sea, and the crisis was averted, but my priorities were revealed. It's okay to have a favorite thing.

I got nothing and I got everything. I ended up in the 4th quarter of my life, far exceeding what I ever anticipated. I can't figure out how I have so much while others got nothing. I was born in this world like everyone else. I feel uncomfortable that many didn't get the privileges that I have while here on earth. I am blessed with good health and healthy children. A lot can be attributed to luck, a willingness to take risks, being born into privilege, and marrying the right person. My responsibility is to make others' lives as beneficial as possible. I was just dealt a good hand. And then I was trumped by someone who says he has five red cards. A helpful fellow player points out they are all diamonds—a flush. There goes my accumulated winnings. Suggestion: don't play poker for a living.

Whatcha got? I got a bunch of friends. I got a great family. Good health. A positive outlook. And a faith in our maker to dictate my future. Everything else is meaningless. As for possessions, make them timeless. Perhaps an heirloom, such as a watch or ring. Keep them in perspective. Nothing is more valuable than a relationship. Thus, don't let stuff get in the way. We have heard over and over again that money and possessions are not the key to happiness. Unfortunately, we all want to find out for ourselves. Enjoy things that are handmade. Think about how your stuff could improve someone else's life, and give it to them. And experience real joy.

The poker game is over. I go home. I got nothing. I lost my weekly allowance of $100. It would have been more fun if I were taking home $100 more than I came with. But the real reason we got together was to enjoy each other's company, create a few good laughs, and have something to remember. Way more important than bragging about winning at the card table. But have I told you about the time I won $400?

Nuts & Bolts: One of our purposes is to see those without as fellow human beings. Doing what we can to make their life better. Think of being generous. Think life-changing. It could be a job, or simply showing interest in someone will help. Nothing feels better than changing someone's life. When it goes well, remember how good it felt. Maybe fold when you have a winning hand. Let someone else take home the pot. Just consider a card game to be like life. Sometimes you win. Other times, it is not a good night. Find joy regardless of the outcome. Bring happiness to others, too.

Story 5:
Double Bogey

We just returned from Ireland. What a wonderful country. Green as all get out. The country is known to be wet, but for our trip, it was generally minimal. However, one day it rained, and boy did we get wet. The locals say you get the whole Irish experience only when it's pouring rain– "when it rains sideways." The wind often accompanies the rain in this country. Most intelligent people would stay inside rather than play golf on rainy days in Ireland. In our case, we had come too far to let the weather prevent us from enjoying the great outdoors. We played on. It was miserable with hurricane-like conditions. Caused a lot of errant shots. But I would do it the same way tomorrow if the opportunity allowed.

Let me start from the beginning. Royal County Down (RCD) is regarded by some as one of the world's finest golf courses. We had traveled across the pond to play on hallowed ground. My golf game does not make me worthy of standing on sacred soil. But the caddy didn't care. He had worked with plenty like me. When playing courses like RCD, you are greeted at the first T [T-box is where you tee off from] by a person who knows golf and the course you are about to play. Kind of a golf Sherpa. You exchange names and carry on a conversation for 4 ½ hours as you walk along the green grass, known as a fairway.

In the USA, we recently experienced a hurricane that tormented the southeastern part of the country, including the area where I live. Floods and wind had left plenty of carnage in our natural surroundings. Unbeknownst to me, the storm raced across the planet and ended up striking the coast of Ireland. The much-awaited day we were to play the storied course was the day the hurricane hit. It was raining sideways, as they like to say. No rain suit could keep you dry in these circumstances. My golf Sherpa told me no locals would ever venture out in a day like this. We didn't care– we were heading out to play golf at Royal County Down. It is the only day we had to enjoy or endure our temporary surroundings. It would also provide me yet an even better excuse for my less-than-stellar play. The grass fairways we had dreamed about walking were filled with streams of water. Our shoes were so soaked that we realized we should have brought waders. And we played on.

One consequence of my particular golf game is that I got to experience parts of the course most players don't. It provided me the privilege of walking on unkept soil called the rough. Yes, this was the result of an errant shot, thus leading to what is called a double bogey.

A double bogey is a frequent outcome of our attempts to put this little white object into a tiny hole. For those not familiar with golf, a double bogey is not a good score. It's two strokes over par on a hole. For the absolute golf perfectionists, this could ruin a day. We golfers live for the swing that inspires your companions to say, "Great shot." And, yes, I can't get enough of those words.

In my case, I have had quite a few ruined days, even though I attempt not to let my mistakes decide the fate of a day on the planet. Perhaps that makes me more resilient to bad news than those low-handicappers. And what is it with using terms like "low handicappers" for the better players? Low typically refers to underperforming. High is generally where we want to aspire. In my case, I enjoy the company of both high-handicappers and low-handicappers. We are all doing the best we can.

On this particular water-drenched day, I was okay getting a double bogey. The weather was outrageous, the course was challenging, and I couldn't see a thing. The fact is, I never had a two-shot above-par outcome. To my chagrin, I watched as the caddy picked up the ball and put it in my pocket and directed me to the next hole. It is pretty discouraging when this happens. While watching professional golf on TV, I had never seen a caddy pick up an errant ball of a professional golfer. But then again, professional golfers manage to stay on short grass away from the knee-high vegetation (unlike me). I don't know how they avoid it, especially when gale-force winds occur. It must not be an accurate depiction of reality. It's more like the professional wrestling you see on TV, full of drama but no real pain.

But there are moments in life when you look beyond the moment. You open your mind to what is essential. Like being awed by the beauty of what is around you. Or enjoying the relationships of those who are traveling with you on this journey. You realize the privilege of life as you reach into your golf bag to find another ball to play. You accept that the circumstances are not what you have chosen, but there is a much bigger picture. You'll never get to live this moment again. Breathe in and enjoy this brief moment. Even if you are soaking wet from head to toe and have endured the embarrassment of having a little white ball picked up and carried.

Heading back home, all I have left are memories. I left several golf balls where they will never be found and won't be missed. I managed a couple of birdies. Several pars. Be mindful that we played a lot of golf. Other golf outcomes: I will leave Ireland with some of my golf balls—those where the ball never got to the bottom of the cup. And I boldly say I had a double bogey. It results from a lack of talent and insufficient practice, I suppose. And from time to time, a little bad luck. I am still pondering why so many of us choose a hobby that has an abundance of failures. Maybe we are gluttons for punishment. Or we can enjoy the company of others as we share this four-hour journey.

There are a few takeaways from my recent experience. When others are struggling, offering encouragement, like 'that putt is good,' is always welcomed. Maybe offer some advice, like, don't swing so damn hard. It's not as pleasant to one's ears, but constructive. Take a moment to look and see who could use your encouraging words. In my case, it sometimes comes from an adjacent fairway. Doesn't matter. Stop your hurried life and invest time in another person. Quite honestly, few experiences are as fulfilling as helping another human being on their journey.

Nuts & Bolts: I had a wonderful trip. I could be a tour promoter for Ireland. My feeble attempts at hitting a golf ball provide great enjoyment. Most importantly, I remind myself that my purpose is to make this world a better place, even when I have to holler "fore" to some poor, unsuspecting golfer. If you're playing golf and have a really bad hole, there's not a lot of motivation to get to the next T-box. The relationships we develop are the crucial reason for continuing. However, hearing you made a birdie or par helps, too. But a double bogey is inevitable and serves a good purpose. It reminds us that life is not perfect, and we rejoice even when it's not. What a great way to live today.

CHAPTER 7

Going Awry Stories

Story 1
I Need Some Help Here

"I need some help here." I heard those words yesterday as my view faded to black: As much as I fought, I could not stay conscious. I was seeing double like I've never seen before. I was clammy. It felt like the flu. I was worried because I've seen others slip into an unconscious state while donating blood, and I didn't want to be that person.

"I need some help here." It came from a nurse or phlebotomist. I remembered nothing else until I came to. When I opened my eyes, a lovely, concerned lady stood by. Several women were hovering about after responding to her call for help. My entourage was visibly relieved when I opened my eyes. In my defense, I completed my blood donation before passing out. I'm not a donating virgin, either. I probably have 150 stamps on my card to prove it. Regardless, you feel inadequate with a wet towel on your forehead and 3 or 4 women in nursing uniforms hovering about. It felt like I was helpless.

Her shirt said, Shannon. I don't believe phlebotomists have stage names, so I believed her nametag. Shannon covered me with wet towels. Brought me a Coke. I told her I was OK, but apparently, my ashen color said something different. I was not being honest anyway. I felt like hell. I couldn't get my eyes to focus. My head was pounding. I was having an out-of-body experience. It feels like a weakness and a lack of control.

It was 5:50 pm. Closing time. Shannon said she would stay as long as necessary. As horrible as I felt, and as bad as I looked, I couldn't help but feel bad for her. It was Friday. She needed to get on with her weekend. She didn't need a 1/2-conscious blood donor victim keeping her from dinner. I felt terrible for those responsible for taking my blood. I was sure they wished I could be patted on the back and sent out the door.

Finally, I convinced her I was OK. I wasn't. I staggered out the door. I still couldn't focus. I didn't know good deeds would cause such problems. I drove home. I didn't hit anybody, but I could have. I staggered into the house, greeted by my loving wife, who asked where I had been. My communication indicated I had control of my faculties. I did not. I should have shown her my bandage, proving I had not met a couple of buddies at the bar. I sounded like I had been out with my buddies based on my inability to walk without swaying or slurring my words, but I was still suffering from the loss of blood.

I was not normal, but normal is not something I often hear about myself.

I had lost control, and control had shifted to Shannon. That hadn't happened to me before. I live in the delusion that I am in control. I never anticipate being out of control. I felt embarrassed. Helpless. I needed the assistance of others, whom I would have never attempted to involve in my life, to come to my rescue. What a weird feeling to be that vulnerable. Do you wonder if people live in that state all their lives? I do.

I've never lost my consciousness like that before. I have had a couple of medical incidents requiring anesthesia. I remember when I was a four-year-old, like it was yesterday—having the gurney rolled down the hallway and going to get my tonsils taken out. I don't know why. They weren't bothering me. My Mom was by my side. Gave me the perception that all was well. There was a moment when my Mom stopped with a look of despair on her face. The gurney went on. A group of strangers surrounded me as I went through a set of folding doors.

A man looked down at me, saying, "You're about to fall asleep." I was petrified. I saw the doctor's face. The screen went black. I woke up in my room with a sore throat and all the ice cream I could eat. I then remember my Mom leaving my room to go downstairs to get something to eat. She told me that she would be back after she got her order. I panicked, and the lady with a child in the bed beside me pushed the emergency button. I can still remember all of the nurses coming into the room. A real old lady, who was probably 35, was leading the way, saying I would be okay. She stayed with me until my Mom returned. It probably was no more than 15 minutes.

I felt the same helplessness with Shannon. It reminds me I'm not in control; I live with lots of delusions in life. The situation with Shannon reminded me that my life is always in the hands of someone way bigger than mine. I want to appreciate that, acknowledge it, and share it with others. I hope to benefit others by being a Shannon in their time of need.

It led me to consider the end of my life in a way I hadn't before. Do I rethink how I live today when I consider there might not be a tomorrow? I feel an urgency to practice what I preach: to care for other people, not with a cold compress, but to meet their needs at a given moment. Provide a meal. Give a ride. Park your car and walk with the neighbor who is strolling down the road. Help a neighbor fix their car - no, never mind, I can't do that.

Now that I'm here and have shared this story, I have got to thinking. Maybe the end is not as far away. I might need to consider what I need to do before my eulogy is read. I might need to write it. Let's make sure today reflects what we want it to be. Moments like this remind us to prioritize what really matters.

Today may be the only day I have. Who knows. The next time I hear, "I need some help here," it could be the last words I hear. In that case, I hope I don't have an IV in my arm. I also hope it is not a policeman saying those words, either. Let me consider what I want my last day to look like. I want to be with my wife- she's a good one. My children, who appear to love me. My grandkids, who definitely do. Some good friends. Boy, I will miss them all— even my acquaintances. I could use a couple of good meals. Don't declare it is one of my last- it ruins my appetite. I will probably want to wander down to the gym. Maybe I can set a personal record for chin-ups. No need to record. I would like some good recreation.

Play golf with buddies. Shoot a score that defies my abilities. I would like to shoot some clay targets or hunt with my dog. Sit down and read a good book. Sit on the porch and enjoy a great conversation. Tell stories. And laugh, in a good way.

Notice I didn't put "complain" on my list. I have a plate full without complaining. I don't want any of the valuable opportunities to be impacted by complaining. I want my eulogy provider or providers to say some positive stuff. I'll write some words just in case they forget. I need to demonstrate care for those around me. It's not hard to find folks who can use my help. I could list many, but I believe we can all find some opportunities to make the world better.

I don't have much time, so watch out. I am a world changer, and I mean that in a good way.

Guiding me back from my unconscious state, my motivated blood-taking team demonstrated some of the actions I needed to take. Of course, they were doing their job. Doesn't matter. I need to address the problems facing humanity and not wait for a knock on the door. I live in a gated community, so this door-knocking is not permitted. I can knock on some doors myself where help is needed.

Nuts & Bolts: Returning to earth after hearing Shannon say, "I need some help here," got me thinking. I'm not in control. I don't live my life with that awareness, but Shannon reminded me that my life is always in the hands of someone way bigger than mine. I want to appreciate that, acknowledge it, and share it with others. I hope to benefit others by being a Shannon in their time of need. And cold compressions will always be included in the list of required equipment for bloodmobiles.

Story 2
It Happens To All Of Us

You walk toward the restrooms. You don't really pay attention to the illustration of skirts versus trousers because you have an urgent need to address. Not thinking, you walk in and head to the stall. And, after you close the door, you realize you made the wrong choice. I'm trying to give you the benefit of the doubt: you were in a hurry. The signage is confusing. UGH. Now, what do you do?

If you had been looking for a urinal earlier, you might have recognized your mistake. OK, enough potty talk.

My son, Gray, had one of those potty identification mistakes. It was his first day as an intern at a construction company. A young intern hopes that his lack of abilities will not be exposed and that his good attitude and promptness will stand out, allowing him to eventually secure a full-time job as a result of his hard work. I'm sure many superintendents have seen plenty of interns show up nervous on their first day of work. I'm sure they were fine having the intern find an alternative way to relieve himself away from the job site. With time, that will change. But for today, Gray's boss permitted him to leave the site at lunchtime.

He chose to use the short time he had to cross the street to a Starbucks to get a cup of coffee. But first, he seized the opportunity to use their facilities. I don't know if you've ever experienced a job site Port a Potty, but they can be challenging. He was not a snob; he simply had the time to improve his options. In our family, we believe that if you are going to use a business toilet, find something you can buy while you are there.

Sometimes, this is a rule, but more importantly, it is a nice gesture.

Anyway, Gray went to the bathroom and closed the door. A moment later, he heard the click-click-click of high heels. He glanced down and saw a black pair of heels with the pantsuit edge resting an inch above the floor. Gray realized the error of his choice, but it was too late to escape. Cleverly, he lifted his feet and hoped for the best. Soon, a second pair of high heels enters, this one blue. High Heel Black starts talking to High Heel Blue. It's probably best not to make any toilet contributions at this time. Meanwhile, have you ever tried to hold your feet up for a significant time? Exhausting.

You might think someone could just walk out, say "Excuse me," admit the mistake, and be on their way. But there is a very real fear that simple ineptness won't be accepted as an excuse. What would these women say if they knew a man was sitting on either side of them? These are thoughts you don't want the answers to. The worst-case scenario? That this was a premeditated act by some creep.

Gray held his breath and prayed for a way out.

Finally, the ladies left. What a relief. He prepared to make his escape. But wait. Here comes another set of high heels entering. Gray might have to spend his whole lunch break in here. Late to work. Fired! Well, it was only a single set of high heels this time. He waited. And finally, the coast was clear.

(And no, I never asked if he washed his hands—probably not.)

Gray sheepishly slipped out of the bathroom, only to spot two policemen nearby. Little did he know that they had witnessed the entire ordeal. They were now wiping away tears of laughter. Gray walked past them, unimpressed with their lack of assistance. Gray decided it was prudent to keep walking out the door rather than ordering a grande. Nobody seemed to notice.

Sitting around the dinner table, we enjoyed the story way more than Gray enjoyed having it retold for the hundredth time. But that is the Rochester way—if there's a chance to laugh, we take it.

Nuts & Bolts: The art of self-deprecating humor is the best kind. Think of stories about yourself that will make others laugh. We all have them. We are better when we are laughing. Just pay attention to the signs on the doors.

Story 3
Running Out of Luck

Sometimes, you're an observer; sometimes, you're a main character. I love to sit around a kitchen countertop and tell this story. My purpose for writing today is to share someone else's story. I am good at it. My son reminded me that the reason I tell other people's stories well is that they aren't always truthful. By the time I finish, I distort the facts so much that the story resembles nothing like reality. I countered by saying that my imagination is far more interesting than reality. Most people agree with my statement. Reality is overrated!

I have documented many of my achievements, conquests, and mistakes. Some of my life experiences have been funny–at least to me. Those who did not find my efforts to make others laugh, I assumed, were in a bad mood. I'll go with that. I recently stood in for a college professor who told me he always has to forewarn the audience before saying something funny, like cueing up the laugh, even if it is not hilarious. In his case, I see why he uses this strategy. He was really boring. Typically, I will stick with spontaneity. But here goes, I'm queuing it up. I am sharing a funny story.

I am glad it didn't happen to me, but I'm happy I heard about it. I thought it was one of the funniest stories I've ever heard. There were several of us around. The sharing of his words made us feel like we were present, leaning up against the chain-link fence, watching our sons practice football, wanting them to be the next small-town hero.

The hero of this story is a high school friend who will remain nameless. We will call him Jerry to protect his identity. And yes, I had a lot of friends in high school; thus, no one can immediately identify my anonymous protagonist. He was an active runner. I don't like the term jogger. It makes it sound like you're barely moving. Running sounds better.

We all start our day not expecting anything out of the ordinary to derail a perfectly good 24 hours. It just happens sometimes. We end up veering off the road. Hopefully, no one gets hurt. On this particular day, our runner, Jerry, gathered with other Dad friends. They attended their boys' high school football practice as they often did. It's a good opportunity to gossip, relive sporting careers, and hopefully see their son make a spectacular tackle or catch a winning practice pass. More than likely, they just killed time, a euphemism for not doing anything really constructive unless gossip is somehow construed as educational.

Jerry used some of his time on the sidelines to get some exercise. He probably didn't miss the conversation much, so off he goes. He was running around the town, and it's a pretty active town with lots of cars. Some folks are walking around outside—a few other runners. But Jerry starts to feel something. He experienced the old stomach-rumbling sensation that all runners have felt at one time or another. This is not just due to having your feet move faster than walking. It's the common upset stomach all living creatures have experienced at inopportune times. Animals may not care very much, except if they are in the house. Then, they have to deal with the pet owner, who is unhappy with the unfortunate consequences.

The reality is that upset stomachs frequently result in expulsions. From where it usually comes in or typically goes out. Awful subject, I agree. The current takeaway is that when dealing with awful subjects, just get to the point. My friend had diarrhea with no immediate bathroom in sight. What could he do but keep running? Alas, pretty soon, a public park is in view, and unlike four-legged animals, he makes a beeline for the public restroom. It didn't matter if it had a skirt or pants on the door. Fortunately, he was correct in the 50/50 chance he had to enter the right door—no need to call the police yet.

And then a beeline to a stall. That is all the details I'm giving you, but let's say it was a success. However, he noticed a minor accident when he looked down at his running shorts, which had underwear built in. As small as it was, he felt obliged to wash out the accident. You would think that was a good decision. Also, he decided it would not be fair to use the sink as a cleaning station out of concern for the future bathroom occupants. Quite considerate. He decided to use the toilet instead. Note to future runners or bathroom occupants: use the sink.

As he dipped the running shorts into the toilet to wash the stain, it would be hard to differentiate which sense was brought into action first. The toilet erupted. He felt the pull of the water as his shorts were ripped from his fingers. He saw his shorts get sucked down the toilet bowl by this modern hygienic device. [I guess the Park Rangers got tired of unplugging toilets and increased the pressure tenfold.] The result was that my friend, a decent human being, was standing in a public restroom, butt-naked. Mind you, he was not a pervert waiting to flash some unexpected restroom visitor. He was a freaked-out Dad with no phone.

This is a real test of resourcefulness. No pants, or underwear, and 3 miles separating you from your final destination. I can only imagine the thoughts that must have been going through his mind and the immediate panic that ensued. Streaking had gone out of fashion a long time ago; thus, this option was out. Asking a bathroom visitor for help was not considered either. Who in their right mind would ever believe this story? And how could they help? Give up their pants? I don't think so. I'm sure my friend wondered how much time he had to solve this problem before he was locked in the bathroom for the night.

As he was pondering options, with a heartbeat bordering on a cardiac event, my friend quickly dashed into the stall when others entered. Fortunately, he detected no other runners experiencing diarrhea. Just normal visits. He was well protected in his 2'x4' stall. Or jail cell. If he had a heart attack, this might be the easiest way out. Or he could claim he was robbed. And they stole only his pants? The lie detector test would be tough.

He attempted a couple of fashionable designs with paper towels, but they did not work, even though my friend is quite creative and resourceful. I wish I could use his name and give him credit, but I still want to remain friends with him.

After what seemed to be an interminable amount of time, Jerry came up with a Plan B, or more likely, Plan X, Y, or Z. He took the T-shirt he was wearing, and thank goodness he was wearing one, for it might have spared him death by embarrassment. He made a diaper-looking assembly with this T-shirt. It took a couple of attempts to make sure the openings did not occur in the wrong place, which would have defeated the purpose. Wearing the T-shirt diaper, he went running back to the haven of his gossiping football practice Dads. Or at least in that direction. I imagine he was running at a record pace, for I know the street he was traveling on and the numerous cars that would witness this spectacle. Some were laughing, I'm sure, while others were appalled. This is not the kind of spectacle Southerners take kindly to.

Can you just see him blazing down the sidewalk, his infamous run of shame, making his final turn into the parking lot? By this time, it's Friday Night Lights, and the entire lot is lit up and visible to all. His friends were lined up along the fence, chewing the fat, relaxed and happy, and they looked up. He doesn't even glance their way as he hauls ass as fast and invisibly as he can to his pickup. One last prayer in the hope that his truck and keys are where he left them. It has been a bad day, but it could get worse if someone helped themselves to his car.

God is looking out for him, for he's able to jump into the front seat and grab his truck keys off the floor. It cranks up, and he's relieved it starts- he'd hate to have to do repair work in this costume. He left his football-practicing son on the field. He could figure out how to get home on his own. A good test of character.

It could have made the local newspaper. The son wasn't aware of how close he came to being involved in a small-town incident. His father could have had his picture on the front page, running in a diaper. The family probably would have had to move, and his son would have had to play for another team. Anyway, it didn't happen. That's the end of the story. I would like to say they all lived happily ever after. They probably did.

Nuts & Bolts: Don't put your shorts near the toilet. I can't imagine wastewater treatment facilities with many running shorts floating around. More importantly, laugh. I've repeated over and over again, we just need to laugh. Why is laughter important for the human condition? It momentarily - it's a fleeting moment - is the most desirable human experience you can have.

Also, tell your stories. Nothing makes you feel alive like telling a story. Especially when you gussy them up a little, like I have been accused of doing. Finally, if you glimpse a poor stranger, butt naked, exiting a stall in a public bathroom, don't hang around to help. I'm sure they will figure it out. Hope you've enjoyed this one.

Story 4
Altered States

I really like live music. It started in 1973 when I was a freshman in high school. I went to the Carolina Coliseum in Columbia, South Carolina, to see The Eagles and a guy named Jimmy Buffett. Tickets were $4.00. In contrast, I paid $450 last night to see the Eagles in Charlotte, NC. Why would I pay so much? Well, music is important to me. When I contemplate which of my senses is most valuable, sight is first. Hearing is second because it has numerous layers. Several sounds are going on at the same time, and they create a heightened awareness. I appreciate it.

Back then, Columbia didn't seem to appreciate Buffett very much. I remember some boos coming from the audience, sounding a bit like a bad call in a football game. He was perceived as country music back then, and people came to hear rock ' n ' roll. It was confusing, but since Jimmy hadn't introduced his line "Wasting Away in Margaritaville," his playlist was limited. Music was one of my favorite pastimes then, and it still is now. As much as I enjoy recorded albums, I like live music way better. Though it started when I was in high school, it really became a passion when I went to college. I recall I stumbled into a small venue to see an unknown group called Pure Prairie League. It starred Vince Gill, and I remember thinking, I might be seeing history in the making. Vince Gill went on to become an Eagle, one of the most significant rock bands of all time, and the first band I ever saw live. Life continued to provide me with circles of connection with music.

Another example involves The Allman Brothers. The first time I saw The Allman Brothers was in 1975, all five hours of their show. The loud arena was filled with a haze from the smoke of cigarettes and illicit substances. The Allman Brothers have always been known for being a jam band that would elongate a song by straying from the musical course, often by playing their instruments. One of their songs would last 45 minutes. Later in life, I'd get tired of Mountain Jam. It gave me a good reason to go to the bathroom and get a beer. On the other hand, Jessica plays for about 15 minutes, and I love it. It gives every band member an opportunity to showcase their skills. Chuck Lavell playing the piano was one of my favorites.

Fast forward almost 40 years. I have a habit of circling dates of concerts on my calendar. One I had circled was October 25, 2014, the last performance of The Allman Brothers. I had circled it 6 months in advance. As the week of the concert approached, I thought harder and harder about taking a road trip to the event. I woke up the morning of the concert, went to my office, called my wife, and told her I was going to NYC. A little surprised, she says, "What's going on?" "I'm going to see the last performance of The Allman Brothers." She says, "You gotta go. Have you asked anyone to go with you?" I told her, No, I was possibly going by myself.

I got off the phone and thought, I should call my friend, Jim. He was a music fanatic as well. He owned his own company. When I called, Jim whispered into the phone, "I am in a meeting." Quickly, I said that I'm going to NYC to see the last Allman Brothers' show. Do you want to go? He whispered, "Get me a ticket, I'll be there." I immediately bought two overpriced scalped tix to the concert. Then I bought airline tickets. With no clear plan, I jumped on a plane, flew to NYC, and arrived at 6 pm, then headed to the Beacon Theater. At 7:45 pm, my working friend sauntered up as if this was exactly how we had planned it. We spent one of the most memorable nights we could have ever encountered.

It felt like the band knew it was their last time onstage, so they went to great lengths to make sure they weren't mailing it in. It was a 5-hour show that ended at 2:45 am. We both had a hotel room with a flight out at 6 am. We passed on the hotel, sat in a coffee shop, and reminisced about enjoying each other's company, knowing we had a story we'd be able to tell forever.

Music provides escapism. It's not running away from your problems. But it's enjoying the moment you are living in. When I hear bands attempting to create sounds that are entertaining and popular, my mind searches for the intricacies of their voices and instruments. It makes me feel like I'm a part of the musical presentation. Feels like a fantasy. Sometimes, you need to experience sounds that transport you away from the difficulties of life. It's an altered state that I embrace.

I enjoy live sports too, but someone usually goes home disappointed. Music events generally leave attendees feeling happy. Some may have gotten too happy and will feel it the next day. I've been there before—it's just the consequence of attending live performances. However, I remember how a sore head feels and have gotten pretty good at avoiding cocktail flu. I do have a history of suffering from an altered state after attending a live concert and then trying to avoid conversations with my parents.

In those teenage years of my life, I had a curfew. I had to get home before the streets were empty to ensure my safety. My Dad always said, 'Nothing ever good ever happens after midnight.' Restriction and curfew were two words teenagers hated. I frequently had some explaining to do when we got home.

I would have been caught a lot more often for underage drinking if Mom had insisted on a proper goodnight peck. She was sleeping, and Dad was not, but he was in bed. I don't know if he was aware of my drunken state. I was pretty good at carrying on a coherent conversation after a night on the town. When forced to provide an excuse for why we had been missing during the dark hours, it pulled on my imagination. Many times, I had to create words that were not exactly as our night had unfolded. This engaged the creative side of my brain, which I still use to this day.

When I was a young adult discussing marijuana with Dad, I was well past using it. Back then, pot was viewed in the same light as Satan worship by the current generation. During my conversation with my Dad, it got to the point where he was about to ask if I'd ever smoked pot. At that moment, I decided to lie and say I hadn't; he couldn't handle the truth at that stage of life. Anyway, he thought better of asking and probably rationalized that it was best not to know. Years later, reflecting on the same topic, he noticed some acquaintances of his smoking pot.

He had anticipated antics like howling at the moon, so he was surprised to observe their behavior become quite mellow. Somehow, he found the courage to ask me if I had ever smoked dope. By that point in life, he was mature enough to accept that this exposure to a mind-altering substance did not permanently damage his 50-year-old son. My experience with smoking dope was brief–I didn't care for the medicinal effects much. I also wasn't fond of the potential consequences of smoking. I decided that alcohol was just fine.

My Dad didn't know what to say. We've all been there, those awkward moments when it's your turn to speak and nothing comes to mind. He muttered something like, "I wonder if Dan ever smoked." Dan is my brother, and he certainly had smoked a lot more than I did. By this time, I believe America had discovered nothing wrong with enjoying a joint now and then. I told my Dad that he would have to ask Dan. That was the end of that conversation.

Speaking of doobies, I saw The Doobie Brothers for the first time in 1975. By then, I was rolling in live music because I had a driver's license. They were an annual occurrence in Colombia, SC. I saw them most of the time when they toured. Then, they played as a backup band for the Eagles in 2024. It was deja vu. Fortunately, this passion, fueled in college, continued into my 60s. I travel across the country to see some of my favorite entertainers. We recently saw George Strait in his final show in Fort Worth. This was my wife's choice. We have been trying to see some of our favorites before we read their obituaries. The Rolling Stones are a testimony to sex, drugs, and rock' n roll increasing life expectancy, but we probably won't live long enough to catch their last show.

I frequently get asked what my favorite show is. The answer I often give is that it's the next one. I always hope that my next loud guitar, accompanied by drums, piano, and a great voice, will be mystical. And magical. I will miss these concerts when I can no longer attend. I can't imagine assisted living centers having a bus to take me to a concert venue. I'm far from needing to consider giving up my live music shows. Since my first concert, I have been a spectator to many rock 'n' roll icons. The performers are now senior citizens, and their best music dates back 40 or 50 years. We still go if they are in town because we thought they needed the money. Rock' n' roll icons back in the day probably didn't have accountants, but likely had plenty of drug suppliers. Maybe they had a handful of girlfriends. We know how expensive girlfriends can be.

Music stimulates my imagination. The way artists craft words and sounds to make us want to listen repeatedly is magical. Some people think music is just noise, and I agree—especially when it's blaring from a nearby car, shaking everyone's windshield at the stoplight. Unless it's classic rock, of course. Then I roll down the window and shout, "Turn it up!"

Nuts & Bolts: Life is short, and I have 65 years of experience to prove it. We are gifted with many opportunities on this earth— some are divinely created, while others are man-made. I'm grateful that I seek out things regularly that I deeply enjoy. My best days are not in the past. I hug my children; sometimes I kiss them too, especially when they arrive late. I suggest you practice your "Have you been drinking?" speech, but don't ask your kids if they smoke marijuana unless you can handle the truth or sense there's a problem. Most importantly, see a live music show tonight or tomorrow night; don't keep putting it off because tomorrow may never come. Remember, we are alive.

Story 5
The Trigger

I enjoy shows and podcasts about murder. Those murder shows typically end up the same way. Some mystery is followed by a tidbit about a girlfriend or boyfriend. It ends with a charge against some unsuspecting person who, for some reason, thought the best way to solve the problem was to take a life, often by shooting someone. Note to those considering ending a relationship: call an attorney instead. Reruns of murder mysteries can entertain me. I don't even need new material. Begrudgingly, I admit I see my share of those 30-minute to two-hour trigger pullers.

I like shooting. At clay targets. Sometimes animals. It involves a trigger. I sometimes struggle to know when to pull the trigger. A loud sound occurs, and surprisingly, the bullet hits where I aim. I never point a gun at another human being. I wish nobody would. I used to shoot paintballs at people when it was popular. Perhaps we could develop a system where potential criminals use paint rather than lead when engaging in violent behavior. It would save a lot of lives and jail time.

A while back, I had several high school classmates visit town, and I was considering another kind of trigger—the trigger of asking a question. At this age, we are all too old to brag about sports accolades and girlfriends. Most of those stories were made up anyway. [My apologies to the girls who were the focus of my imagination.] It is funny how something we haven't thought about in decades can be jarred to the forefront of one's mind by a comment or question. Often, a thought from our past is way more important than the stuff we have been collecting in our brains. My old friends and I discussed occurrences we have not remembered in decades. Sharing our stories was quite enjoyable. Except when someone reminds me of an embarrassing moment in which I was the main character.

Some triggers can be life-changing. I recall being asked by a friend, Ron, a question that prompted me to take a long, hard look in the mirror to answer truthfully. Ron wasn't even a close friend. I am sure he had no clue how his six-word question would impact my life going forward.

A little context here. I have loved a lot of things about my life. One aspect of my life I fully enjoyed was my career. I loved working. And was rewarded for it. The more I worked, the more money I made, and the more I heard clients say, You can always count on Tom to be there when you need him. It was nice to hear. I talked a lot about my work, too, a characteristic Ron recognized when we were together. I remember walking out of church on a sunny spring afternoon with Ron. I assume we participated in some small talk, but I can't remember. I was thinking about how I would spend the rest of my day. Kind of wished it was raining, so when I went to the office, I wouldn't feel like I was missing much. As Ron walked beside me, I do remember him asking me the question I had not pondered: Why do you work so much?

At first, I denied that I had worked too much. Then I went on a rant, stating that to be the best, you must sacrifice whatever it takes to achieve the unreachable goal called "best." I sounded like a Marine recruiting commercial. In other words, I shared with my nosy friend that I had to work so much. Then I shared that, thank you, I still had time to spend with my kids, make it to church on Sunday, and half-listen to my wife. He wasn't impressed. Long story short, he pulled the trigger. I started thinking that maybe I should reconsider how to spend my limited time on earth. I decided I needed to make some life adjustments. All because I was asked a trigger question.

I faced the fact that it's not normal to spend Saturdays and Sundays in the office. I decided to spend my time addressing the life that had been ignored. I changed my attitude and decided that being booked over capacity is not a permanent state of mind to live in. Slow down. I didn't even need a traumatic event in life to cause me to alter my journey. Spending time on neglected relationships became my priority. I still worked plenty. Just not irrationally.

When I came home from work, work stayed in the office. Previously, when my kids went to bed (sometimes before), I would pull out my briefcase and start working on things that could really wait till the next day. Vacations were no longer semi-work trips in which I carried my computer and fax machine to signal to my customers I was still at the office. Mustered the courage to say, "I'm on vacation. Can this wait until Monday?"

Another example. A friend, who was being semi-interrogated about his faith, didn't defend his thoughts on faith. Instead, he asked the interrogator, "What do you believe in?" This initiated a dialogue rather than an argument. I found his example really useful for addressing uncomfortable topics. We need to work hard to see what unites us instead of what divides us. Sometimes, a question can resolve conflict. Other times, a question can jar a memory or a recollection of a great time in someone's life.

In conversations aimed at unlocking memories of the past, I prefer to focus on the positive ones—there's no need to bring up divorce or jail time. Some thoughts should remain blocked if you genuinely try to help someone remember. It's like one of my poor decisions, which I won't mention here. Other memories need to be coaxed free. Consider assisting a friend by showing curiosity, not nosiness. There's no need to inquire about their W-2 or sex life.

Nuts & Bolts: Today, in your human encounters, seek to help your fellow humans by assisting them in reflecting and remembering. You can even seek out people to help you do the same! Volunteer history about yourself, too. The trigger to remember and reflect is in your hands.

CHAPTER 8

The Ties That Bind

Stories on Family

Story 1
Wild Horses

I am the patriarch of a horse family. This was not my choice. It started innocently enough. My daughter, Haley, was not gravitating towards activities like sports or dolls. I remember her first-ever effort playing soccer. It was a YMCA soccer team, not one of those time-consuming, energy-infused travel teams. On the opening day of the season, as Haley was chewing a braid of her hair, the other children chased the ball. She stayed as far away from the action as possible. We knew her soccer career was over before it started. Every parent seeks to find a place for their child to fit in both in the educational world and with hobbies. I was always amused when raising children, how we parents seem to work into the conversation about how gifted our children are. I remember hearing stories about kids reading at three. Or hitting a baseball at four. The Rochester's were pretty average. We just wanted our kids not to wet their pants before heading to preschool. Thus, finding the skills of the youth was a little bit of a project.

Haley's first exposure to a horse didn't go well. It was her first cousin's birthday party. She was 4, and her younger brother was 2. The pony was the main attraction. I don't think Haley ever got on and even cried a little, as I recall. Her younger brother wasn't afraid. He kept getting in line to sit on the reluctant animal as the owner dragged him around a circle. Her brother had way too many interests, and horse riding would not be added to the list. He would have to wait until another kid's birthday party to ride a pony, for it would not be his own.

We once again encountered horses on a trip to the beach. We were killing a little time on a hot afternoon. Haley seemed enthusiastic, so we headed out to a shady farm advertising horse riding. I was paying for this pony walk, and I wanted her to stay on until the time was up. She stayed on the horse for a good 30 minutes. I was tickled because it appeared to be something she enjoyed, while my other attempts at creating hobbies had not excited her.

Upon arrival at home, Cindy, who served as wife, mother, and advocate, said riding lessons were starting the following week. I paid no attention, which was typical of me. I assumed it would be a phase that would pass quickly, like many other efforts. In general, when negotiating with the children's promoter, stall as best you can. Pushing back just makes one dig in deeper. You can have the whole family against you if you're not careful. Instead of filibustering, just say, "OK, OK, whatever you say. I give in."

The lessons started. One day, I showed up at the stable to see what the hullabaloo was all about. I was surprised to find Haley was good at it. Unlike soccer or basketball, she was an active participant instead of a faraway observer. I was pleased, but waited for the comment that the riding experiment was over. It didn't happen. The next thing I knew, a subtle hint about leasing a horse was made. I didn't know you could lease a horse. Leasing a car or a home, yes. Horse leasing was a new concept.

I asked a client who was in the horse business what it meant. First of all, he tells me, no one's in the horse business. There's no business. Just expenses. He told me this was a real problem. For example, he suggested I get a second job at the Circle K kind of problem. I had a good job, but it didn't leave me enough time as it was. He said you will have a major investment in this new hobby in a heartbeat. I protested - there's no way this could be correct. Both of us were wrong. It cost our humble household way more than he estimated to participate in this endeavor.

Leasing may be a solution for avoiding the expense of owning a large, expensive pet. In reality, it is a gateway to horse ownership. There is no avoiding it. I understood that you train a horse to be more valuable and then sell it once your child outgrows it. Wrong again. The animal is yours in perpetuity. We had ponies that lived to be over 40 years old.

One was written up in our will for survivorship. Not only do you have to keep them, but in my case, I bought a farm so they could live out the rest of their lives in a happy place. My wife said once you own them, you must look out for their well-being forever. Till death do us part. I haven't checked the law books, but I assume it is in there somewhere.

Meanwhile, Haley continued to develop as a competent rider and showed a willingness to care for the stall inhabited by a 1200-pound animal. Horse conspirators struggle to be completely forthcoming when participating in dinner conversations. I sat having dinner with my family for months, cryptically hearing my teenage daughter mention Brady.

Finally, assuming this was a boy she had a crush on from school, I asked her to invite Brady over sometime. She looked at her mother, and then turned to me and said, "Daddy, I can't bring Brady home. Brady is my new horse." My jaw dropped as I looked at her mother. She quickly responded, "I told you about Brady, and you were not listening." I didn't listen a lot, which is true.

But if I were, I would've wanted to see a Brady business plan. See how much money I was going to lose. Or invest. I would like to call myself a horse investor. However, from an investment strategy perspective, I would likely have more success buying crypto currency coins than horses.

Haley got so good that she started competing. You have to have a trailer to haul the animal around. Then, you have to have a vehicle to pull the trailer around. The cost of ownership has nothing to do with the price of the horse. My original hope was that the horse hobby costs would be curtailed when you bought the animal. Not so. There are boarding fees, riding lessons, and vet bills. Trips to riding events.

A job at a convenience store will not come close to covering these necessities. I should have gotten the soccer ball out again. This is beginning to sound like a rant. It is meant to be a warning of sorts. It is an educational piece for generations to come. The lesson is simple: listen. Meanwhile, my daughter had become a competent and confident rider. It taught her excellent life skills. I am proud of her.

The problem expanded. Cindy's 40th birthday was approaching, and I noticed odd body language. The kind that says we have to talk, but I don't know how to start. I was pretty sure she didn't have a boyfriend. I asked her what was up. She mentioned her 40th birthday would arrive soon.

This was undoubtedly starting better than what I feared hearing, like "I am moving out." I assume some lovely jewelry or a new car was in the asking. She deserved it—some noteworthy gift. I want a horse, she said. I revert to my tactic of slow-playing the passing thought. My answer was something like, Sure, we could talk about it. She holds up a picture of Nantucket—her newest acquisition. I didn't even bother to say, Shouldn't we have discussed this first?

It wouldn't have gone well. I have made some significant purchases without consulting the financial committee, too. It was hard for me to argue about expenses. She hates it when I tell the story, but I feel safe writing it because she doesn't read my scribblings.

[**Editor's note:** Cindy didn't read this story, but she overheard us discussing it. She is adamant that her version of the story is the correct one. She remembers that Tom reached out to Cindy's trainer, asking how to buy Cindy a horse. Tom had agreed in advance to buy Nantucket.]

So, I believe we now own five horses or ponies. The line has always been blurry as to how many horses we own, and I'm okay with that. I see how much joy it brings Cindy, and therefore brings me joy as well. First, there was Flicka, then Trey, Brady, maybe Blueberry Muffin, and Nantucket. Oh yeah, Pippin. To tell you how bad I am at recognizing these horses, I'll share this story. Cindy and I were at our farm in Aiken. She told me to fetch Trey from the pasture, who I knew was a white horse. I walked a few hundred yards into the field, and two white horses were standing before me. I'm trying to figure out which is which. I tried calling for Trey to come to me, but unlike dogs, horses don't respond to their names. I notice they are wearing jackets (which Cindy calls blankets). One says Trey, and one says Nantucket. Easy! Proudly, I grab the horse wearing the Trey jacket and march back to Cindy. She's looking at me quizzically, and I don't understand why. She says, "That's not Trey." I tell her, "Yes, it is! It says Trey on the jacket." She says, "Horses don't read." Apparently, any jacket can be put on any horse. This further confirmed that I have no understanding of what it is to be involved in the horse companionship arena.

Twenty-five years later, I'm still the reluctant groom in the stable of life. My wife's heart belongs to her horses; I'm just the stable hand. I have the diversions, too—expensive ones. We have several horses that appear to be capable only of eating hay, being led out to pasture, and then returning to the barn. They are not rideable or sellable. They are just big pets. At least they don't howl at night. They do make a mess in the pasture. Cindy still loves to ride. Haley has hung up her gear for motherhood. She is on to many other lessons. I wouldn't trade the ability to watch the feminine side of our family enjoy the horse experience for anything. We can afford to have these pasture ornaments.

Nuts & Bolts: I love my wife. She loves horses. I guess, in a way, I love horses too. My intent with this story is to make fun of myself. Never in my wildest dreams did I think horses would become such an integral part of the Rochester family. A horse and its companion have proven to be great educators. Haley and Cindy have both benefited by virtue of choosing this stall-mucking hobby as their use of their time on this planet. By the way, when you hear unfamiliar names mentioned at the dinner table, ask questions. And listen better. It may prevent you from being surprised by the addition of a new and expensive family member.

Story 2
A Walk In The Woods

I wanted to figure out why our anatomies were different. I played doctor with another four-year-old girl out behind our house. Nothing sexual. She and I did find some discrepancies. Somehow, I thought she was left without, and I didn't make a big deal of it. There was no need to hurt a child's feelings. What I did discover is that I enjoy the woods. All went well with my friend until our mothers discovered poison ivy in awkward locations. We lived in an area of South Carolina where poison ivy and poison oak are as common as pine trees. Some folks who were highly allergic had to live elsewhere. I grew pretty immune to the itching red bumps that cursed many other aspiring young doctors. Our moms told us not to study each other's anatomy anymore; the hospital was closed. I still have some questions, though. Mom said she would tell me later. I figured it out myself, with help from one of my friends and the girly magazines we found in his Dad's closet.

A few years later, my brother, Dan, and I started playing army in the woods, protecting our community from Germans and Japanese. I don't know why we never watched out for the Vietnamese when that was the war going on at the time. Maybe we were conscientious objectors. Or weren't allowed to watch the news? Instead, we built forts and gave ourselves ranks. We made plans to camp out in our forts. But never did. A Mom would holler in her gentle voice, Time to come home, and we slept in our warm beds. At 9:00 AM sharp the following day, we would continue our surveillance. I guess we relied on the police to take the overnight shift. I never saw any foreigners. Only moms and dads wanted to see what we were up to.

And then came my teenage years. The woods became a refuge in our attempt to grow up. It started with drinking beer or sometimes liquor borrowed from one of our Dads' cabinets above the refrigerator. For some reason, my Dad thought it was out of our reach. Maybe the insinuation was that it was out of our reach. I never got caught with my Dad's stash of Jim Beam. He wasn't a big drinker, so I had to be careful. I would dilute the proof by adding a little water and tell myself I protected him from getting inebriated.

The woods continued to be a favorite destination even after I grew up. There is always so much to think about. It's pretty quiet. There's a lot to do to figure out the arrangement of all the trees and other vegetation. I worked as a forester's assistant in college. The first instruction he gave out was to keep walking if you come across dope fields or liquor stills. If someone is around, stop and act like a curious college kid. Not hard for me to do. My colleague and I stumbled on a liquor still on the first day of the job. Two old men were cooking distilled spirits. I did what my boss told me to do. I sat on my ass and learned to make alcohol, and I got paid to do it. It was a great day for a walk in the woods.

I had great summers working in the woods as a forester's assistant. My favorite was getting lost. Many times, I was stuck on dirt roads, and once, I was on a railroad track that could have been ugly. There is something about me that I don't turn around. I just keep going. It's not necessarily a good characteristic. Sometimes, I have been known to make three right turns and then left just to avoid turning around. You'd have to be there, but you have two choices when faced with a muddy waterhole on the road. Plow ahead or turn around. Thus, I got stuck a lot. In this era, there was no Triple AAA. No cell phones. We would walk a mile or two back to the paved road and start looking for help. Inevitably, we would find some farmer with time on his hands. He would get his tractor and pull us out. Sometimes, the farmer would haul us around and show us his crops, his property lines, and his house. And he even introduced us to his wife. But only to introduce. Southerners also like to show off their belongings to others from the South. Non-southerners would be stuck in the woods until AAA and mobile phones were invented. I just happened to be born at the right time and the right place.

Nuts & Bolts: The woods are such an incredible part of my life here on earth. I am still wowed to this day by my experience in the woods. I like them better than my cozy surroundings in front of the TV with a chair that fits just right in a 70-degree room. The outside is the way our world was created. It's funny how most of us have abandoned what we were meant to enjoy while here. The takeaway is to get your rear end off the couch. And find time to spend outdoors—one without walls but with a ceiling full of blinking lights. Be on the lookout for red bugs and poison ivy. Keep your clothes on unless you have the opportunity to have a companion who is a nature lover. And, of course, watch for low-flying planes.

Story 3
Hello, Hello, Hello,
Don't know why you say Goodbye,
I Say Hello

As I approached the building, I realized I was in conversation with myself. *I cannot get these words out of my head: "Hello, Hello, Hello, don't know why you say goodbye, I say Hello." Everyone has had a song that somehow managed to control their thoughts. I hate it when the song stuck in my head is not a favorite. However, "Hello, hello, hello" really resonates because it emphasizes the importance of greeting each other energetically. When we do not receive an energetic response, or in the case of the Beatles song, when we receive a rejection, we struggle to understand why. Why would someone ignore or reject an enthusiastic greeting?*

I've always had an aversion to revolving doors. I stepped carefully and walked through this one without stumbling or stopping as it turned around. *There are endless versions of the greeting "Hello." Two common ones are "What's up," and "How are you doing." I like the latter. Sounds folksy. I like sounding folksy. It makes me feel approachable. It kind of forces someone to respond. Unless they are really in a bad mood, or maybe I did or said something in a prior segment of my life. Have I mentioned my memory is short? I can't possibly consider what may have happened to prevent someone from receiving a warm greeting.*

Once on the other side of the revolving door, I looked at my phone, for what reason I just didn't know. Then I headed down the corridor and focused my attention on a door. I'm sure I ignored all other faces in the course of my travels. Typically, when people pass me, I work really hard to make eye contact. Don't know why I have that habit. I attempt to share a moment of acknowledgment as we pass each other. "Hello" might be one of them.

But the opposite of hello is goodbye. In airline stewardess speak, I guess saying goodbye is pretty permanent. Our relationship lasted from takeoff to landing. I can't imagine how those men and women tolerate humanity sitting in a seat waiting for them to make the flight more comfortable. If I were one of these caregivers, I would have pointed to the many food stores throughout the airport, which can provide numerous choices of gastronomic fulfillment. I would say, now sit your ass down, buckle your seat belt, and don't bother me or anyone else until you feel the wheels hit another tarmac. I wouldn't be very good at representing an airline. I'll take a Diet Coke and pretzels, please.

I walked 20-30 yards and turned left, and could see the door I was looking for. I assumed a more serious and fearful demeanor. I found myself bracing to hear words that I didn't want to experience. *Other goodbyes can be terminations of sorts—many versions. Like, get the hell out of here, or are you done? It's hard to follow up on that with a future "Hello." But sometimes, we need ways to end a conversation abruptly, not my forte. I am too polite. I should have been assertive a few times. Southerners historically gravitate to politeness. We have been known to let telephone solicitors go through their whole spiel before saying, "No, thank you." We are obligated to thank someone for calling in the middle of our dinner and telling us we need a new credit card or a car warranty. Or have DirecTV tell me in an automated voice that I can get 50% off if I push a button on the phone. I want to ask why they don't cut their price by 50% and advertise this outstanding bargain. Instead, I just hang up. I guess that is a way of saying goodbye. I don't feel bad hanging up on an automated recording. Now, back to my dinner.*

I was close to my destination. *"Love you" is a pretty nice way to go your separate ways. It makes you feel like there's more to the relationship than just a conversation. I would be wary if a stranger were to utter these words. It is a little early in the getting-to-know-you stage to find out that this person you met online is ready to go to the altar. Let's stick with people you know. Saying you love them. It might be the most appropriate way to say goodbye. It's almost the equivalent of a "hello, hello, hello," which you know I love.*

Well, I arrived. In the hospital room. With my brother. Who is in the ICU. On a ventilator. Praying that this is not goodbye. Realizing that we will all say goodbye to this world someday. I'm kind of sad thinking about it. There were some miracle workers there. Hopefully, they could perform one on Dan. If not, I will say goodbye. But there will be a day when I can say, "Hello, hello, hello," again, I believe.

Nuts & Bolts: Now that I think about it, you can never say I love you enough. Keep saying it.

Story 4
Dan and Feeling Your Pain

I am fortunate. At 65 years old, I can only claim a few aches and pains. To my credit, I am great at letting the world know when I am feeling an ache or pain. It's so great that I'm not sure I could tolerate a competitor. I have a lot of friends with new knees, hips, and shoulders whose function is to relieve the pain. Sometimes it does. However, there are several forms of pain. Physical pain is the worst for me. You just can't get away from it. Fortunately, a lot of pain is part of the healing process. It helps you remember not to repeat what hurt you in the first place. It's a pretty good system. Thank God for that.

Pain is an excellent reminder of our humanity. Without it, we can get pretty oblivious. It almost makes us feel invincible. When we are fortunate to go extended periods without pain, we tend to get reckless. We can start feeling apathetic towards those who suffer pain. I don't encourage you to invite pain into your life. Things like walking on hot coals or pulling out your fingernails come to mind and sound like a form of torture. Life is painful enough without inflicting it on yourself. Torture creates pain of historical proportions and can be used to interrogate. Approach me with the threat of torture, and I'll tell you everything you want to know immediately. I'll spill the beans, and you can save the electricity. The danger of being sent to my room as a youngster got the same results. I'm warning you, don't tell me a secret.

Right now, I am feeling a different kind of pain. It's hard to explain, really. I would appreciate some good suggestions on how to deal with it, but from my experience, you have to deal with it yourself. This kind of pain is between your ears—not a headache. Maybe it is a different kind of headache.

I lost my brother today. It wasn't as if he had wandered off, and I needed to find him. No, it was the day of getting the phone call. You know, the phone call. I was in a room traveling with three friends to one of America's greatest golf courses. I had my shorts, golf shirt, and hat properly matched for the day. I was tying my shoes, and I got a phone call from a friend. I was talking to a friend when I saw a call coming in from my sister-in-law. I clicked over and she said three words, "Dan passed away." The world stopped. This opportunity to play golf - great as it was- just didn't matter. I had to come to grips with losing my brother. With his passing, I had no members of my immediate family still living, and it hurt.

"Dan passed away." It wasn't completely unexpected, but it still makes you feel like you're jumping out of your skin. Can you sense it? I had to take a deep breath. Losing a loved one brings a different kind of pain. Since it's so fresh, I feel like I have a heavyweight on my chest. I don't understand why—there's nothing but air in front of me, plenty of oxygen to breathe, yet I can't catch my breath. It also makes tears flow from my eyes. As a child, I felt the need to suppress my tears. It was seen as a masculine trait. I can't recall it being taught in school, but among my peers, a common question after an accident was, "Did you cry?" Sometimes, I don't understand why God created crying. It embarrasses me when I well up like I'm weak. What a silly perspective, I know. Tears aren't physically painful unless you're peeling onions or eating jalapeños. But those are topics for another writing day.

I started thinking back to the 61 years we shared on the earth together. He was a younger brother. My Mom said I was so bossy to my younger sibling. As we grew up together, we shared a room; he had the bottom bunk and I had the top. Seniority mattered in our room. We bonded like most siblings who shared a 14x10 space—rarely had any major fights. Then I began thinking about high school and what came afterward. Dan was always funnier than I was. I was funnier when I was around him as well. I also say that, as hardworking adults, we both suffered from the decision not to prioritize our relationships with those we should have. We were two brothers who did not spend much time together. But that's not abnormal. Life gets in the way. We both had children. Before his passing, we spent quality time together that I won't forget.

He's now not available to tell the stories that were so important to our family, to create laughs, to tell disparaging stories about my ineptness with the shotgun, or when I shocked him with a cattle prod. Dan had a nature about him that he inherited from our Dad. He could talk to anybody. His daughters would say the same thing about Dan that Dan and I said about our Dad, which meant that he could not avoid a conversation. It was a caring approach to a conversation. He won the trust of others in a way I never saw with anyone else, except my Dad. I gravitated to chasing girls and balls in high school. Dan and my Dad spent time fishing and hunting together. In retrospect, I wish I had spent more time with Dan and my Dad as they pursued their common hobbies. When he died, Dan had a lot of outdoor friends.

It's painful to think about how we will never be together on earth. The freshness of losing a loved one makes you look at the loss others experience with more compassion. Those newscasters and writers reporting on senseless deaths now serve as reminders of someone else's loss and their pain. I hate the senseless loss of life. I'm a big fan of creating an eradication plan for needless suffering.

I know I'm not alone here. Everyone, or anyone who lives outside a bubble, loses someone they love or care about. Dan was such a great guy, a great brother, and a great Dad. It's the kind of stuff that makes for a heartfelt etching on a tombstone. But he was much more than a great guy. He understood the quest to make this place better than you found it. I am not talking about just picking up litter. Dan knew we had to enrich others' lives. And he did. Everyone who came in contact with Dan walked away a better person.

As a result of today's phone call, I am stuffing my suitcase to return home. I have gathered a few observations: All life is precious. Remember to reach out to the sufferers. A big hug works wonders. In our family, we were very loved. But we were not a hugging family, nor did we exchange verbal "I love yous." I felt so loved as a child, but it was expressed differently.

It is hard to come up with the right words to console others. "It was God's will" is the wrong one to come out of your mouth. Nobody said that to me, thank God. A note is fine. I quite honestly didn't want to talk about Dan not being here. Not today. I definitely don't want to find fault in anyone attempting to console me verbally on day one. I have just found myself struggling to talk. My emotions rise, and tears flow. It just hurts, not like a sprained ankle. My voice cracks. I can't spit out any sensible words. Kind of embarrassing, actually. I discovered that when you see someone grieving, it is an appropriate time to ask, Is there anything I can do? Or, can I get you an Uber to the airport? Or better yet, take them there. Or take care of their dogs while you are making funeral arrangements. If you reach out, your timing might be perfect. Care or love can be expressed in simple ways. When love flows, sparks fly. Not like the 4th of July. Way better.

So today, add this to your task list: "Find someone to love." Words from an old Crosby, Stills, Nash, and Young song. That phrase makes a great song, but it's better when made into an action. Don't walk a wide swath to avoid someone suffering. Just walk up to that friend or stranger and say, How can I help? Say it like you mean it.

Nuts & Bolts: Tell all your family that you love them. Friends too. I haven't said it nearly enough. There were many times when I could have said it to Dan, but I didn't. I never faced the reality that the day would come when I heard, "Dan passed away." You will never regret saying, "I love you." Let's start today.

Story 5
Best Day Ever

First of all, grand parenting is a lot of fun, at least for Cindy and me. There is a reluctance to let me grandparent by myself; I have a reputation for letting my grandchildren do more than they would with their parents. Maybe I allow them to eat dessert before a meal or climb a tree they were ordered to stay out of. The reputation is well-earned. But I hope all humans get to experience being around youngsters when they are in the golden age of life. None of my children lives anywhere close to our home, so when they come to our home field, we want to take full advantage of our time together.

All this to say, Cindy and I were a little anxious when our 1,500-mile-away grandchildren were making a trip to see us. This may sound selfish, but we wanted the week to be so much fun that they couldn't wait to come back. Hopefully, the parents will feel the same. So, we planned one activity after another. Major stage productions require less thought than the level of planning we put into their daily activities. Secretly, we wanted to be the A-Team of grandparents. I don't believe this is an official title; it's just the first number called when the grandkids needed a sitter.

Thus, Camp Rochester was formed in Aiken, South Carolina—horse country—a place we call our second home. Cindy was determined to create a perfect week filled with activities that would never be forgotten. It felt nostalgic for me. I have vivid memories of family trips from childhood, yet I can hardly recall what I ate for lunch yesterday. It's funny how that works. We were hoping to create memories for our grandkids that would live forever. I was wondering if we could pull it off.

Do you remember what it was like when you were young and in awe of the world around you? Aging somehow makes us less amazed. But spending time with the grandkids allows me to recapture that youthful magic. What an incredible way to make us all feel truly alive again.

In preparation for the upcoming get-together, we went a little overboard with planning—or really, Cindy did. Barnum & Bailey Circus would have been upstaged. We borrowed animals and arranged trips, including a ride through the zoo and a trip to the movies. My grandson's favorite stop was the county fair, where he rode every ride on the property. The faster, the better. He was only 8. I easily met the minimum height requirements, but was reluctant to get on a ride that made me feel like throwing up. Mason couldn't get enough of it, while my granddaughter, Mary, insisted on winning something. I spent $50 winning a $2 stuffed animal, and I was her hero. We all went home with blue faces from cotton candy. I guess we should have saved it for after dinner. When comparing it with all the technology at her fingertips, there is no substitute for the Himalayan running in circles backward or bumper cars banging into each other.. They just can't be improved on.

The movie trip is always a great stop. We ate as much popcorn and drank as much as we could stuff in our mouths. I was a huge fan of this stop, although I had to visit the bathroom three times in the one-and-a-half-hour movie. There were horseback rides. Eating out. Endless activities. Nothing was off the table.

Of course, not everything went according to plan. Nap times got in the way—sometimes the kids needed a rest, but more often, I did! "Grandpa, again?!" There were a couple of rain showers, clearly beyond our control. But as the sun set each day, we were all worn out, which made us think that maybe, just maybe, Camp Rochester had been a success.

A few days in, we sat around the breakfast table, and one of the kids started chanting, "Best day ever!" Soon, everyone joined in, and we were all yelling in unison, "Best day ever," laughing ourselves silly. It was magic. And just like that, "Best day ever" became our mantra—our new way to start each day. I believe we did it! We created forever memories.

That experience moved me and got me thinking. What if we approached every day with the mindset that it would be the "Best day ever?"

For me, spending quality time with my wife is at the top of the list. I'm sure conclusions are being made, but I want a different quality of time. Meaningful conversation would be pleasant—a couple of laughs. Belly-aching laughs will be even better. The list should have started with a great cup of coffee and silence. I understand that a workout can be punishment for some, but I enjoy going to the gym. Maybe I'd close a big sale at work or get a promotion—that could certainly make for an excellent day. What would your list include? I challenge you to try it: make a list of what would make today the "Best Day Ever" for you, and see if it brightens your day.

What about those days when nothing is going right? I have a story about a day I anticipated would not be the best. Or even good. This story was filled with surprises.

Contrary to what Hallmark would have you believe, I don't think wedding days are the happiest day ever. That's a myth. A wedding is an event that you endure, not for yourself, but to bring happiness to a lot of guests, many of whom you may never see again. This was not going to be a good day.

You might shed a tear as you watch the newlyweds walk the gauntlet, I mean, the aisle, to get to the escape vehicle at the end of the ceremony. Hallelujah. Let's be honest; you're just glad it's over. Until, of course, the bills come. They haunt the parents long after the last dance and are relieved that the financial bleeding has finally stopped!

I got married over 40 years ago, and it was a beautiful day—a small town affair in a little Methodist Church, followed by a reception at a Southern mansion. A mansion where I come from didn't have to be that impressive. It's not like Tara in Gone with the Wind. The "mansion" is pretty modest by today's standards. Since then, I've watched three kids join their mates in holy matrimony. Fortunately, we all made the right call on compatible human beings, so the result was positive, but let's face it, the actual wedding days aren't what I'd call the best. That was until my daughter's wedding.

It was at her wedding that I experienced an amusing turn of events. It wasn't because of the over-served guests–though I have a few great stories about them. I pulled one of the young men or victims of alcohol over-imbibing out of the bushes. He said he was just tired — that's what I told the search team that had spent an hour looking for him. It was pretty entertaining. No, this time, the surprise came courtesy of Mother Nature herself.

My wife hired a choir for the ceremony, and let me tell you, they were phenomenal. Did I mention I had wanted to stick to a budget? I imagined checking costs and comparing the budget to actual expenses. If I had any intention of running this wedding like a business, my wife did not get the memo. Paying an entire African-American choir was not part of my vision of saying, "I do." They were good. And I was reminded over and over that it was only money. Code for: you can't stop it anyway.

So, here we are in the middle of a beautiful outdoor wedding. Our daughter and her husband had just exchanged vows and were walking away, hand in hand, ready to start their new life. Unbeknownst to us, a black snake had slithered its way into the choir area. The next thing I knew, there was more hopping around than at a trampoline park. I mean, it was like popcorn popping in hot oil. Like a house on fire. At first, I thought they were just excited about my daughter's wedding. Maybe hit the bar a little early. I thought it was part of the act. Then I realized it was something far more dramatic. Those who have never experienced a black snake were not enjoying the moment. The choir members were in panic mode, scrambling in every direction and hauling ass to their automobiles.

Once I heard the facts, I looked at my two sons to determine their level of guilt. But no – this wasn't their fault—just good ol'Mother Nature making her appearance.

That does not constitute the "best day ever," but it did provide one of the most memorable moments of the day. My takeaway is that every day has the potential to be the best day ever. You just have to choose to make it so. And I'll even include wedding days, I guess.

The "best day ever" is a philosophy. When entertaining our grandkids, I decided it was worth starting every morning with the declaration, "Best day ever." Why? Because today is all we got. That's it. Living in this imperfect world is a privilege, yet we often take it for granted, assuming tomorrow will come. But there will be a day when it doesn't.

So, consider my philosophy: Best day ever. Think about it while showering, drinking coffee in the morning, sitting behind your desk, driving the kids to school, or going to school yourself. Whatever you're doing, don't waste it.

Here's what I think will happen: morale improves when everyone buys into the idea of making the day great. Heck, turn the music up—play "We Are The Champions" and maybe even bust a couple of moves! This attitude also reminds us that life is finite. There's no time to waste. Even if yesterday was declared the "Best Day Ever," today is brimming with opportunity. Just seize it. I'm already levitating with excitement! I'm committed to making today the best day for everyone around me. And I can't wait for the next visit from the Grandkids. And then, their weddings!

Nuts & Bolts: I am asking for help here. Let's spread the word. We are all put here for a purpose: to live in the moment and make it unbelievable. Go out and make it the best day ever.

Reflections by the Editor

"Tell me the facts and I'll learn. Tell me the truth, and I'll believe you. But tell me a story, and it will live in my heart forever." - Native American proverb

Tom is a natural-born storyteller—someone who knows how to entertain while quietly delivering insights that stay with you. There's a beautiful honesty to his voice: warm, funny, sometimes a little raw, but always real. As I read through his stories, something unexpected happened—I began seeing my own life a little differently. My thinking cleared. My days felt more intentional. Without even realizing it at first, I began to feel better. This book was quietly helping me become a better version of myself.

When I read these stories, I don't worry about perfect punctuation or polished prose. Instead, I settle in and let Tom take me on a journey. His words come straight from the heart, and if you let them, they'll speak to yours.

Tom has a gift for making you laugh out loud and then, in the very next breath, making you think. Just when you're chuckling at some ridiculous mishap, he'll gently turn the story inward, toward something authentic and meaningful—something you may have forgotten but needed to hear. The lessons he shares aren't new—things like, "You can't take it with you." But hearing them wrapped inside a hilarious tale about losing at cards somehow gives them new life. Tom's stories are full of those little winks from the universe—the kind that catch you off guard and stay with you.

I don't see his reflections as advice. They're more like gentle nudges in the right direction. In that way, this book becomes a kind of moral compass—a friendly guide for finding your footing in a world that can feel unpredictable and overwhelming.

If Tom had one wish, it would be for everyone to write their own stories. He found deep value in looking back, reflecting, and putting his life into words. He'd love to know that his stories encouraged someone else to do the same.

These days, when the world feels heavy and uncertain, I find such comfort in stories like Tom's—stories that remind us of what truly matters. They bring us back to the basics: slowing down, laughing more, loving deeply, and living with heart. Ultimately, it's all about people and relationships. Tom gets that. And he invites you to remember it, too.

~Joey Xanders

Acknowledgements

"Acknowledgment" doesn't quite hit the mark for what I want to say here. It sounds too much like someone standing at a podium, rattling off names after winning an award. This isn't that.

This is me wanting to say thank you to the many people who've contributed to my life and made it possible to put it down on paper. First and foremost, my wife, Cindy; my kids, Haley, Drew, and Gray; my Mom and Dad –thank you for your love, your support, and for being my foundation. And then there's a long list of friends - some I'm lucky to have still close, and others I miss from earlier chapters of my life. I won't name names, only because I know I'd forget someone, and I wouldn't want to leave anyone out.

If you've made it to the final pages of this book, I'm especially grateful. Your time and thoughts mean a great deal. I'd love to hear what parts resonated with you, and any ideas you might have to help me grow as a storyteller. One of my main hopes in writing this was to encourage others to share their own stories– for their families, their friends, or even just for themselves.

I really would like to thank my editor, Joey Xanders. She has taught me a great deal about storytelling and writing, and even more about the power of encouragement. It kept me moving forward when the ink felt like it had dried up.

To anyone who has spent a little time with these pages, thank you. Let's keep the conversation going. There are more stories to tell, and I look forward to sharing the ones that didn't quite make it into this round. Our relationship is to be continued.

Joey would like to acknowledge her generous family members and friends who spent time with the manuscript, providing thoughtful feedback: Jan Coonrod, Sarah Cunningham, Michelle Freeman, and Dara Greene. She is very grateful to Andrew Juris for stepping in when she needed help. Thank you!

About The Author

Tom Rochester was born and raised in Lugoff, South Carolina. He attended Clemson University and earned a degree in civil engineering. Shortly after graduating, he married his wife, Cindy, and together they moved to Dallas, Texas, for work. After three years with a Fortune 500 company, Tom decided it was time to pursue his entrepreneurial dreams.

He relocated to start his own business—a specialty materials company serving the commercial construction industry. In 1985, Tom and Cindy relocated to Charlotte, North Carolina, to establish Southeastern Architectural Systems. Over time, the company evolved into a subcontracting firm providing cladding systems throughout the Southeast.

Soon after settling in, Tom and his wife began their family. They have three children and are now proud grandparents to six wonderful grandchildren. Tom especially enjoys making "Camp Rochester" a fun and memorable destination for the young ones.

Following his recent retirement, one of Tom's first personal projects was writing this book. He and his wife have also embraced their love of travel. A shared passion for live music often shapes their travel itinerary as they explore the world together. Some of their favorite recent destinations include Croatia, England, Ireland, Argentina, Vietnam, and Portugal.

Tom has a deep appreciation for the many opportunities life offers. Writing is one of his greatest joys, along with speaking to groups to encourage others to make every day "the best day ever." He finds particular inspiration in connecting with younger audiences.

His other passions include engaging in thoughtful conversations, golfing with friends, and hunting with his dogs. He also enjoys staying active at the gym. Above all, he cherishes time spent with his wife—especially sharing stories and laughter.

About the Editor

Joey Xanders is the founder of The Story Road. Together with her team, she guides people through the process of uncovering, preserving, and sharing the stories that define their legacy. Whether it's a book, podcast, or film, The Story Road captures and shares life stories in a meaningful and authentic way.

www.thestoryroad.com

www.ingramcontent.com/pod-product-compliance
Lightning Source LLC
Chambersburg PA
CBHW051148120626
46547CB00012B/997